BROAD SEA AND
EMPTY SKY

BROAD SEA AND EMPTY SKY

CHINA'S GREATEST MODERN POET
Xu Zhimo

DOROTHY TRENCH BONETT

FLOATING WORLD EDITIONS

Contents

Publisher's Note

Dorothy Bonett's translations of Xu Zhimo's poems have appeared in *Delos: A Journal of Translation and World Literature* (Volume XII, Number 1–2, Summer–Winter 1999, pp. 54–60; Volume 33, Number 1, 2018 pp. 24–25) and *Lighted Corners*, the literary and arts magazine of Mount Saint Mary's University (2004–2007, 2010–2011), and have won an Honorable Mention for the Der-Hovanessian Translation Award given by the New England Poetry Club in 2006. *Cambridge, Farewell Again* appeared in *Torch Magazine*, Winter 2016, along with a brief article on Xu.

A version of the essay on Xu Zhimo as translator was presented as "The 'Tyger' in China: Xu Zhimo's May Fourth Translations of Poems from Foreign Lands" at the Mid-Atlantic Region Association for Asian Studies conference held October 24–26, 2003, at the George Washington University. Some of the material from the introduction was presented in a paper titled "A Lyric Fusion: Xu Zhimo's Use of the Old in His New Poetry" at the Washington Area Traditional China Colloquium held in May of 1999 at the George Washington University.

Some translations and commentary were also presented at the American Literary Translators Association conferences in 2017, ALTA40, "Reflections/Refraction;" in 2019, ALTA42, "Sight and Sound;" and in 2020, ALTA 43, "In Between."

Dates

Poems are dated [in brackets] as reliably as possible, usually based on publication in book or magazine format, but sometimes from dated diaries or correspondence, or by the poet's own notation, in which case there are no brackets.

ACKNOWLEDGMENTS

There are many people I would like to acknowledge for their help and support during this project, which has played out in a manner that has been providential in the true sense of the word, over a period of many years. My journey with Xu Zhimo began in the late 1990s, while I was an adjunct at Mount Saint Mary's University in Emmitsburg, teaching Chinese language. Dr. Martin Malone of the Sociology Department, who was teaching *Bound Feet and Western Dress* (the memoirs of Xu's wife Zhang Youyi written by her grandniece), asked me if the protagonist's husband was an important Chinese poet. I had never heard of Xu Zhimo at that time. My studies in Chinese poetry at Yale, in France, and in Taiwan had been confined to the classics and I knew little about modern or contemporary poets in China.

When I mentioned Xu Zhimo's name to Chinese friends, however, they were very enthusiastic, and many could recite (or sing) excerpts from his work. It was clear that this was someone of great cultural importance. Yukchun Yu Mastandrea shared her favorite works of his and I fell in love with what I read. I started to translate the poems for Dr. Malone's class, and did this for many years. I want to thank Yuk, and Marty, and his students for their initial encouragement and enthusiasm, as well the staff of *Lighted Corners* (the Mount's literary magazine) where my translations first appeared.

I began to share those translations with colleagues at the Washington Area Chinese Roundtable, and at the Washington Area China Colloquium where about twenty years ago I met Dr. Jonathan Chaves of the George Washington University. Thank you, Jonathan, for your encouragement over the years, your belief in these translations, and especially for your example. You are one of the main reasons that this collection is seeing print. The other person who has been of key importance is Karen J. Gillum. Karen, you were always willing to read or listen to a new translation; to discuss it at length; to encourage me when I needed it, to make suggestions and also to tell me honestly when things just didn't work! I value nothing more than your keen critical sense and your good ear—except your friendship. Over the past year, Cynthia Chuiyuen

Yung has been willing to discuss the obscurities in the Chinese text and to offer helpful suggestions, and has shared much about Chinese culture that can't be found in books. Thank you, Cynthia; I value your knowledge and I am glad we are friends.

My husband of thirty-seven years, Michael Bonett, who is my best and most constant supporter, has not only been patient about a lot of work and recently, a lot of deadlines, but has always gone above and beyond in order to help. Not many spouses would have been willing to go book-shopping in Beijing in the 1990s with long lists and questions for staff in a completely foreign language.

Of course, none of this would have been possible if I had not myself begun to study the frustrating, difficult, marvelous Chinese language, literally a lifetime ago. I need to thank Mamie Tsang Foote for deciding that I was going to do this, when we were in high school together, and nagging me until I gave in. Cynthia Green Warren (1958–2020) was my constant companion in my studies and set a shining example. You are missed so much, Cynthia. I also had many inspiring teachers, at Yale, at l'Universite de Paris VII (Jussieu) and in Taiwan, including Vivienne Lu; Zheng Chouyu; Hugh Stimson; Parker Po-fei Huang; Jin Bilan and of course my advisor for my master's thesis, Yu Ying-shih. 一日為師, 終身為父. But I have always been fortunate in my teachers. I was first encouraged, not to write (I was doing that from a young age), but to show my writing to others and to publish it, by Frank McCourt at Stuyvesant High School, a very kind mentor to a very timid student, in school and afterwards.

In Taiwan, I also became friends with John Wu, Jr., and Terry Wu. John is the son of John C.H. Wu and I thank both the Wus for all their encouragement and kindness and John for allowing me to read his memories of his father's friendship with Xu.

It is not just *xiào* (filial piety) that makes me acknowledge my parents, Grayson Trench (1930–2000) and Lucille Clark Trench. Immigrants to the U.S. from Belize, they not only valued and encouraged my education, but never once questioned my choice of Chinese language, literature, and history as course of study, back in the days when it was not only unusual for a young woman of color to make such a choice, but for anyone to do so. The U.S. did not have diplomatic relations with China at that time and Sinology was a very esoteric choice of vocation. But my parents were not afraid of unusual choices. Both of them loved literature; my mother and my grandmother (Nina Heath Clark) loved English poetry in particular. They instilled this love in me from a very young age. My mother, who at age eighty-eight can still recite long poems by Wordsworth, Keats, and Coleridge from memory, also has two brothers who are poets. Branston S. Clark of Cambridge, Massachusetts, a modern poet who writes in English, taught me to understand and respect contemporary works. I grew up with the music of his poetry in my ears. Ronald L. Clark (1935–1988) was a poet who was interested in the pioneer writers in Belize Creole (Kriol) and because of his work I knew something about the arguments for and against writing in a vernacular.

I cannot end this list of acknowledgments without thanking my publisher and editor, Ray Furse, who not only believed in this project enough to take it on, but has done so much to make it what it is. He encouraged me to translate many more poems than I otherwise would have, kept in touch with me while I was doing it, and his sensitive editorial suggestions have all been improvements. He is of course not responsible for the flaws that remain. During the last phase of this project I have also been extremely privileged to be in contact with Tony S. Hsu, Xu Zhimo's grandson and author of a biography about him, *Chasing the Modern*. Tony has been incredibly generous and kind, given up a great deal of his time, shared information, provided valuable feedback, pointed me to additional resources, and provided rare illustrations. I have valued our conversations and appreciate his knowledge, his quick wit and his precision.

Most of all, though, none of this would have been possible without the help of God, who brought me through some difficult places to get to this point. I want to append to these acknowledgments the motto of the Society of Jesus, who were the first great Western interpreters of the West to China, and of China to the West, as I learned in my work for Yu Ying-shih.

AMDG

—Dorothy Bonett, 2020

China's First Great Modern Poet

Everyone Wants to Fly

On a foggy night in November of 1931, a plane crashed in Shandong Province, China, killing everyone on board. Besides the crew, there was only a single passenger. Not many people chose flying as a means of transportation during those early days of aviation in China.

The passenger had flown often, though, and he had often used flight as a symbol of personal freedom and individual happiness in his writings. Those writings were read avidly by members of his generation, who wished for these two things as ardently as they wished for freedom and independence for China. "Everyone wants to fly," he had written. "It is so tiresome to be crawling on earth all the time . . . Who does not dream of soaring up in the sky to watch the earth roll like a ball in infinite space? . . . That alone is the meaning of being a man."[1] The young people who read those words might not have been able to "soar" themselves but could feel as if they were doing so when they read about his voyages to exotic lands like Germany, Italy, England; when they followed newspaper reports about his travels around China as the interpreter for the Bengali poet Rabindranath Tagore; and when they read his poetry in the iconoclastic "new" style.

Now, however, he had crashed like Icarus (a figure who would not have been familiar to his readers). He lay, a burned and battered corpse, somewhere in the vicinity of Mount Tai, one of the Five Sacred Mountains of China. When his remains were recovered, he was buried under a massive stone that read simply "Grave of the Poet Xu Zhimo." He was only thirty-four years old.

The nation mourned—for a while.[2] Then China underwent one drastic upheaval after another—civil war, invasion, civil war again. The country split in two in 1949. The bulk of it, the mainland, was after that date in the hands of a regime that did not care for poetry (or literature in general) unless it

1

served utilitarian purposes—that is, unless it was propaganda of the most fla-grant kind. Xu became *persona non grata*. His poetry was not printed; when his name did appear in histories of literature, it was stated that he was a "reaction-ary bourgeois poet and playboy whose works must be criticized and opposed."[3] Finally, during the Cultural Revolution, the Red Guards punished his legacy for literary crimes. His books were burned, his cemetery monument smashed, his grave was dug open, his remains scattered.[4]

Then came a reappraisal, and a renaissance. After the end of the Cul-tural Revolution in 1976, his poems again took the place in China that they had never ceased to have in Taiwan and among overseas Chinese, wherever there was literacy in Mandarin. His works were published in edition after edi-tion; scholars began to study him; his poems not only became required read-ing for students, but his popularity burgeoned. His gravestone was found and restored. And then, in July 2008, another monument to him was erected on the other side of the world, on the banks of the Cam River at King's College in Cambridge, England, where he had spent the best year of his life. Soon, over a million Chinese a year were visiting this new monument, which is a simple stone, inscribed with words from his best-known poem. Taking note of this, Cambridge began to pay homage as well to this famous alumnus, hitherto unknown to them.

Left: Xu at Clark College, Worcester, MA.
Above: The Chapel and Gibb's Building of
King's College at Cambridge.

So Xu Zhimo became an icon at the ancient British university that he had attended, admired, and made famous in China. In addition to the 2008 memorial stone, the China-UK Friendship Garden (also known as the Xu Zhimo Garden) was inaugurated there in 2018.[5] A poetry and art festival is held there in his honor every year, and at least a dozen translations have been made into English of the poem that is partially inscribed on the monument. The *Second Farewell to Cambridge*[6] is now quite well known, so some non-specialists in the West have become aware of Xu as the author of this single poem. Specialists, of course, know of his complete *oeuvre*, and a couple of excellent studies of it have been done In English. A few other poems have been translated. Biographical material has been published. But there is no way for Westerners to come to grips with his enormous, influential legacy when the bulk of his work has not been translated into any European language; addressing that lack is the purpose of this book. Through these translations, the largest number of his poems and prose writings available in English at this time, I hope to introduce Western readers to the man who is loved, respected and acknowledged, in China, as "China's first great modern poet."

Xu Zhimo Garden at King's College, photo courtesy of Jeffrey Tse.

The Chinese Hamilton

Xu Zhimo[7] was born on January 15, 1897.[8] He was born into privilege (his father was a successful banker), and he was wealthy for most of his life. He was, however, born in a time of crisis and change in China. The Boxer Rebellion was defeated in 1900, when he was three years old; he was seven when the age-old civil service examinations were abolished and the educational system in China changed entirely; he was fourteen in 1911 when the Qing dynasty fell, ending five-thousand years of imperial rule. And when he was

3

twenty-two, the disgraceful Treaty of Versailles made it clear that the European powers and Japan would continue to trample on a weak China, as they had been doing for almost ninety years.[9] Versailles granted to Japan the Chinese territory that had "belonged" to defeated Germany. Chinese representatives were not present when this was decided, and the resulting outrage led to what is called the May Fourth Movement.[10]

Xu was not present in China when students rose up and began this protest movement, which was to have far-reaching effects. However, he was absent because he too wished to "change" (that is, reform) China."[11] He was in the United States, part of a large (and diverse) group of Chinese studying abroad; their goal was to acquire Western knowledge in order to fix problems at home. Xu was studying economics at Clark University (then Clark College) in Worcester, Massachusetts, and aspired to become the "Chinese Alexander Hamilton," going so far as to take Hamilton as his English name before departing China.[12] He had also taken on a new Chinese name. He had been named Xu Zhangxu at birth, but now he took Zhimo as his "courtesy name." One biographer suggests this is because the meaning is possibly "intending to do everything for the benefit of mankind and wearing himself out thereby."[13]

Xu Zhimo and and Zhang Youyi in France, 1921.

In spite of his youth, Xu had married and had a son before he left China. As was the custom at that time, his parents arranged a marriage to Zhang Youyi, a girl from a well-connected family.[14] It was only after the birth of this grandson that Xu's father allowed his son to go abroad. Probably, as Gaylord Leung suggests, the father and son had different goals in this from the beginning—the elder Xu thinking that the foreign study would be good for the family, while the younger considered the nation more. In any case, everyone expected Xu

Zhimo to excel. He had shown great promise throughout his school career, in both traditional Chinese and Western subjects. And Xu did do well. He graduated from Clark with high honors in 1919, and went on to Columbia University, where he received an MA in Political Science in 1920. After that, he left the United States for England.

Xu wanted to study with the philosopher Bertrand Russell, a man he greatly admired. He believed that Russell was teaching at Trinity College, Cambridge, and he intended to matriculate there. It turned out that Russell was not in England at this time, and was no longer at Cambridge. Xu enrolled in the London School of Economics.[15] While he was there he met political scientist and philosopher Goldsworthy Lowes Dickinson, and the two became friends.[16] Dickinson was able to arrange for Xu to come to Cambridge after all, since he was a fellow of Kings (another college at that ancient university). Xu enrolled as a post-graduate student. He did not study economics, though.[17] He had decided to become a poet.

Ah, poet!

What caused this change? To Westerners, a career as a poet seems totally antithetical to one in economics—the latter practical, the former unrealistic, idealistic, even elitist. A traditionally minded Chinese, however, would not have thought this way. As Michelle Yeh explains in her seminal work on modern Chinese poetry,[18] in traditional China poetry had been held in the highest esteem. This was a belief "sanctified by Confucius in the *Analects*, where poetry came first in the 'three-part curriculum' . . . In the political realm, poetry was a practical means of advancing oneself in the world, since literary skills in general were essential for passing the civil service examination, and poetry . . . had been a required subject since the early seventh century."[19] This had all changed with the abolition of the civil service examinations in 1905. Although writing poetry had "ceased to be politically desirable,"[20] many Chinese of Xu's generation still felt that poetry would have a key role to play in China's modernization.

Xu certainly thought so. It is clear that at Cambridge, he was thinking not just about poetry, but about the poet's role in society. In *Dewdrops on Grass*, a poem that has been preserved from his early writings there (p. 41), he addresses the poet directly (*Ah, poet!*) declaring that such a person ought to be:

> . . . first to sense the spirit of the age.
>
> . . . the one who must integrate action and thought.
>
> . . . the one who must forge the boundary between man and heaven—

The poet was also, he went on, "the philanthropist who knows the essence of poverty's source." The word "philanthropist" is a slightly misleading translation here. Xu is not presenting the poet as a social reformer. He is describing a prophet, a seer, a sage—a modern version of Qu Yuan of the Warring States period, who lived from approximately 340–278 BC. This widely admired Chinese cultural hero wrote the great poem *Li Sao*, or *Encountering Sorrow*, and then drowned himself in either protest or despair over the governance of his state. His death is still mourned and celebrated during the Dragon Boat Festival each year. He is one of many examples throughout Chinese history of men who used poetry to attempt to set the world right, just as Confucius had suggested, and Xu clearly wanted to be part of this tradition. He still wished to "change China" using this age-old method, but chose to modify the medium. He was going to write poetry—but not traditional poetry. He was going to write *xinshi*, or "new verse."

"New verse" was very new indeed in 1921. It was part of a broader movement to write in the vernacular language, called *baihua*, as opposed to *wenyanwen*, the classical, literary language that had been used by the elite for millennia. This literary language can be compared to the Latin used in Europe during the Middle Ages. However, it was not "dead" nor was it "fossilized," as the reform-minded dramatically proclaimed; it was terse and elegant and well-suited for many purposes. Poetry was one of them, as the long history of masterpieces in the classical language attests. However, *wenyenwan* took years to learn and was very far removed from the everyday colloquial language that everyone, including the elite, actually spoke. Reform-minded scholars like Cai Yuanpei, Chen Duxiu, Li Dazhao, and Hu Shi had been pointing out, since about 1915, that if China wanted a place in the modern world, it needed a widely literate population, which meant that it needed language reform —and that this was urgent. Strides had been made, and successful *baihua* prose had begun to be written, including vernacular fiction. In 1921, Lu Xun published *The True Story of Ah Q*, still considered a masterpiece. There were good essayists, too, and one of the best was Hu Shi, who had formulated the rules for writing *xinshi* in 1917. Hu Shi's "Eight Don'ts"[21] listed in his 1917 article, "Suggestions for a Reform of Literature" were of the greatest importance and he published in 1920 what was probably the first book of "new poems," *Experiments*, allowing him claim to the title "father of modern Chinese poetry." Others experimented during this period as well, but wrote nothing that an audience who had grown up imbibing Li Bai, Du Fu, Wang Wei, and Su Dongpo and other classical poets found palatable. By the time that Xu Zhimo decided his vocation would be writing new verse, people had actually begun to say that *baihua* and real poetry were incompatible.

Xu's own early efforts in the genre were not successful, in his view, and he destroyed most of them.[22] So it is not known what his first attempts at the genre were like, or how much poetry he actually wrote during the time he spent at Cambridge (1921–1922). This was a key period, however, in his development. It was at Cambridge that he first realized his love of nature, a subject that he would continue to write about during his entire career. Cambridge is beautiful, and the sensitive Xu appreciated that—he later would make his Chinese readers appreciate it as well. More important, however, than his experiences punting on the river, or cycling and walking around the college "backs,"[23] were his encounters with British poets, both dead and alive. The interest that he developed in Keats and Shelley, Byron and Wordsworth, caused him later to be stereotyped sometimes as a Chinese imitator of them—"China's Keats," "China's Shelley."[24] I believe, however, that the living British writers he met at this time had even more influence on him.

Xu half-jokingly described himself as a "hero-worshipper"[25] and it is in this light that his seeking out of writers like Katherine Mansfield and Thomas

Hardy is often seen. Critics express wonder at the way he can describe the strong influence that someone had on him that he only met (in Mansfield's case) for twenty minutes—in Hardy's for not much more. However, I would describe these visits as more akin to "pilgrimages." Xu was seeking a form of enlightenment, and like a religious disciple seeking a master, he pursued individuals whom he believed to be "poet-sages."[26] They were prophets, a vanguard for the betterment of all society though their self-actualization. This can be seen in the "elegies" that he wrote for them, describing their impact on his own work and life. Hardy is described as an old man who "dared not relax. He lifted ideals high." He did this to uphold "the dignity of thought."[27] His *Elegy for Mansfield* (page 163) goes much further. In it, as he grieves for her death, Xu asks the deepest questions about death—and life. And in it, he reaches what he describes as "enlightenment" (in the Buddhist sense) about the meaning of life. His later prose would be very much marked by her influence, as his verse is more influenced by Hardy than by any other poet (something that Cyril Birch explores in his seminal essay).[28]

These writers, mentors in spite of themselves, ineradicably marked Xu. This was, however, a two-way street. Xu met and socialized with people like Roger Fry, Arthur Waley, Lytton Strachey, H.G. Wells, and E.M. Forster, as well as the luminary who had attracted him to Cambridge, Bertrand Russell, who became a good friend.[29] "Here was a Chinese scholar studying at one of the finest of Western universities at a time when Europe and America were questing for knowledge about China. He offered an unpredictable perspective to most conversations . . ."[30] In his Chinese *changpao*, which "curiously half-covered a pair of Western-style trousers,"[31] Xu was undoubtedly personable—and intriguing. Pearl S. Buck would describe him, some years later, as "handsome and rather distinguished . . . He was . . . tall and classically beautiful . . ."[32] If Buck admired Xu, others, who did not have her familiarity with Chinese people and Chinese culture, were fascinated. E.M. Forster, for one, described his meeting with Xu as one of the most exciting things that had happened to him.[33] It would be interesting to see further research done on these relationships between Xu and the English intelligentsia during that pivotal year.

The First Western Divorce

Xu left England with the three-fold faith in "love, freedom, and beauty."[34] The three were all linked in his mind, especially love and freedom. This was not entirely beneficial, however. The most notable way that he sought his "freedom" while in England was through his divorce from his first wife. This was "the first Western-style divorce in China."[35] Traditionally Chinese men of Xu's class who did not care for their wives would simply take concubines. They were of course, like Xu, all in arranged marriages, which had usually taken place when they were quite young and had never before met their wives. This sort of marriage could be very happy.[36] But it could also be miserable, and many Chinese at that time thought that the system of arranging marriages was one of the evils of the old feudal society. Quite a few May Fourth figures disentangled themselves from marriages of this sort, but no one as publicly as Xu, who touted his divorce as an example that would help to "reform society" and "achieve well-being for mankind."[37] It is worth noting that in the West at the time, outside of the rather bohemian circles in which Xu moved, divorce was rare and also not well thought of.

As Xu's wife Zhang Youyi later pointed out, though, the "noble" act of divorcing her (Xu had deserted her while she was with child) would have been more impressive if Xu had not been so anxious to be free for another reason. He was deeply in love with Lin Huiyin,[38] daughter of the Chinese envoy to the League of Nations. He had met the Lins, father and daughter, in London when he first came to England, and rushed the divorce through so that he could quickly marry the young girl. Lin, however, did not marry Xu but rather returned to China with her father. She later would enter into an arranged marriage with the son of Liang Qichao.[39]

Once he knew that he had lost Lin,[40] Xu began the pursuit of Lu Xiaoman, a society beauty who was also a talented musician, painter, and amateur opera performer, but was already married. In a glare of tabloid-like publicity, the two very modern young people proclaimed their right to be together, and their right to "freedom," even though this relationship was even more scandalous than Xu's original divorce.[41] After a couple of tumultuous years, in 1926 Lu

Xu with Lin Huiyin in Beijing, 1924.

Xu marrying Lu Xiaoman in Beijing, 1926.

Xiaoman married Xu. Unfortunately (and predictably), after the marriage took place, Lu didn't see why she was not still "free" to move on, when she tired of Xu and felt attracted to another man. Her extra-marital affair with Weng Ruiwu, which seems to have begun very shortly after the wedding,[42] made Xu miserable in the last years of his life. The whole tangled situation captivated the public imagination at the time and still is an important part of Xu's legend in Taiwan and China. It is safe to say, however, that ninety years later the initial interest would certainly have died down, were it not for Xu's fame and the fact that the three women he was involved with all expressed their views in letters, diaries, memoirs, and poetry.[43]

It is hard to say whether Xu's reputation has been helped or harmed by his romantic entanglements. It is interesting to know the story as an aid to understanding some of the poems, including some of the major ones, but those are far from his only important works (and *Cambridge, Farewell Again* is not one of them). In my opinion, Xu would have been as important to Chinese literature had he remained married to Zhang Youyi.

Sunrise on Mount Tai

Xu returned to China from England in 1922 and plunged at once into the literary scene. When Rabindranath Tagore visited China in 1924, he served as the Bengali poet's chief interpreter. Tagore's worldwide fame at this point was unsurpassed, and he was very much admired in Asia. He had won the Nobel Prize for Literature in 1913—the first non-European to ever do so, and the first person of color. His poetry compilation *Gitanjali*, written in Bengali and translated into English by the bilingual poet, was emmensely popular. The Nobel Committee had stated that the prize was awarded "because of his profoundly sensitive, fresh and beautiful verse, by which, with consummate skill, he has made his poetic thought, expressed in his own English words, a part of the literature of the West."[44] Chinese intellectuals, however, were undoubtedly more interested in the "skill" with which Tagore had invented a Bengali vernacular style in which to write poetry,[45] analogous to what they wanted to do with Chinese vernacular and using *xinshi*; and that his poetry had reached the less literate Bengalis of the lower class in the form of song.[46]

Tagore was also a well-known activist for Indian independence.[47] In 1921 he had founded the rural collective of Sriniketan in his state, in order to effect social change and alleviate poverty in India.[48] Xu Zhimo personally, however, was probably most interested in Tagore's view of the role of the poet. Tagore, as the Bengali would later state in his talks in China, felt that poets were one of the hopes of the world and that their role should be "capturing on their instruments the secret stir of life in the air and giving it voice in the music of prophecy."[49] This was precisely what Xu had imagined when he wrote *Dewdrops on Grass* back in England. And so, before he even met the Bengali poet, an excited Xu published *Sunrise on Mount Tai* (p. 176) to herald Tagore's advent.

This essay is as interesting as *Dewdrops on Grass* and can be considered a companion piece to it. It begins with Xu standing on the summit of Mount Tai, looking out at an endless "cloud ocean," waiting for the sunrise. The cloud ocean is vast and formless and described in words that imply a primordial void. As he looks out at the "cloud essence," Xu's body starts to metamorphose, "to grow to a limitless size; the mountains underneath my feet give shape to my torso." But the body is not Xu's any longer. He is instead looking at a "giant, with . . . disheveled hair, [who] stands on the mountain peak and faces the East, stretching out his long arm."

The giant is clearly Tagore, and although the Bengali was extremely tall, the size refers to his moral, rather than physical stature. Tagore had long, white hair; and his name in Chinese, Taige'er (泰戈爾), has as its first character the name of the mountain, Tai. But the giant is more than Tagore—it is the ideal poet as hero, poet-sage (which is why Xu at first feels that he himself is metamorphosing) and it brings to mind Pan Gu, the original being, the Chinese Adam. This becomes clear later in the essay as the giant's "body of myriad colors stretched out on the limitless sea of clouds" begins to "vanish in the universal rejoicing," his "magnificent ode . . . also becoming again imagination, in the bright clouds." Pan Gu was not just Adam, the first man—he was also the creator. But to create he had to die, and then his corpse became the sun, the moon, the mountains and rivers—the wind came from his breath and animals from the fleas on his body.[50] Just so, the giant in Xu's work lies down and disappears—and the "ode" that he has created "penetrates everywhere."[51]

This mythic aspect of Xu's essay is as important as the philosophy that is also contained in it. The giant points to the East in the poem, because "from the East comes a . . . universal brilliance, to bless us all—appearing—arriving—here—" and because the East, if it "rises up" and "exerts its strength" can have "victory" and "resurrection." This mirrors Tagore's belief that China and India, if united, could surpass a Europe waning in greatness, so long as the East did not trade its more "spiritual" values in exchange for the West's "destructive" materialism,[52] (displayed in not only in the Great War, just past, but in the artificial Western values). Many Chinese agreed with this, and Xu was certainly interested in this idea (although he clearly did not feel that Britain, as exemplified in Cambridge, was given over to materialism). Others, however, passionately disagreed with this "Pan-Asianism" and with the idea that China had anything further to learn from India. (After all, they already had

Xu and Lin Huiyin with Tagore in China, 1924.

Buddhism, seen in some quarters as an integral part of the failed traditional culture.) Tagore's talks in China drew crowds of adoring admirers—but there was also strong opposition. Progressives, especially the newly formed Chinese Communist Party, not only passed out leaflets that mocked him but disrupted some of his speeches so that they could not be heard.[53]

Thus, Tagore's visit to China was not entirely successful (and Pan-Asianism never took off). Xu, however, remained awed by the Bengali sage. He wrote an essay after the visit was over in which he said that Tagore could not "be surpassed, he is a mysterious natural phenomenon."[54] Xu had finally found the role model he sought, and had also found a mentor, a friend, and father figure. Tagore (who was sixty-four years old when he came to China), was very responsive to the eager young man. From the first, he treated Xu as if they were family, noticeably favoring him over the other members of the group who welcomed him to China.[55] "Tagore immediately recognized in him first of all a fellow poet, secondly a man with a sense of humor, thirdly a man through whom he could get in touch with the spirit of the Chinese."[56] Xu kept up a correspondence with him, and went to India to visit him. He wished to found a collective in China modeled after Srinitekan, established by Tagore in Bengal. As for Tagore (who would outlive Xu by many years), he came to China again twice, unofficially, to visit his friend.

Xu had his hero, his role model. Now he had to complete the task that he had set for himself back in England. In 1925, he published his first book of poetry, *Zhimo's Poems (Zhimo de shi)*.

Cover of Xu's first volume of published poetry, Zhimo's Poems.

14

The Poems

A Lyric Fusion

Why is Xu Zhimo called the first great modern Chinese poet? There were other excellent poets who appeared at around the same time. Many were friends of Xu, which was not an accident. He surrounded himself with people of talent, and in 1923 he founded the Crescent Moon Society.[57] This society, named after a book by Tagore,[58] is one of the most important groups in the history of modern Chinese poetry. The list of luminaries who were members is long, and includes names like Wen Yiduo, Zhu Xiang, and Rao Mengkan. These poets of the beginning period of modern Chinese poetry not only encouraged and influenced each other, but laid the critical foundation for everyone who came after them.[59] Xu was the center of the group, which fell apart after he died,[60] and was very involved in many of the group's endeavors, including the magazines and books they published.

As stated earlier, the Chinese had been pursuing the goal of writing poetry in the vernacular since 1917. Hu Shi had stated clearly what it should *not* be like, but it was not so easy to say what it *should* be. The first vernacular poets were confronted, as Michelle Yeh points out, "with the predicament of mas-

Logo of Crescent Moon Bookstore, established in 1927.

tering a new medium in order to create a prosody suitable to it."[61] This would have been a difficult job in any case, and was especially difficult due to the nature of classical Chinese poetry. Although it is not the impression one gets from English translations, classical verse in Chinese is governed by many rules. It always rhymes, and which words can be rhymed with other words is inflexibly determined by what rhymed in centuries past.[62] The number of characters in each line determine the meter and the tones, even and deflected, and must be arranged in a strict pattern.[63] The classic poets also used a set poetic vocabulary, including many allusions, that this highly educated group and their elite readers all knew. In short, the poems in this tradition are actually more rigidly organized than Shakespearean sonnets or medieval French rondeaux.

So, perhaps naturally, when freed from all the rules that they were used to following, (as well as from the requirement that they write in an archaic language) modern poets foundered. Most of them "wrote whatever was on their minds" in exactly the same way that they would have spoken it "and passed it off as poetry."[64] By 1919, the critic Yu Pingpo was reminding them that "to write vernacular poetry is not to speak in the vernacular; the difference . . . may not be apparent but . . . it is there."[65] This is because their results, as Julia C. Lin points out, when "compared with the great legacy of traditional poets . . . appeared awkward, crude . . . immature."[66]

This cannot be said about Xu Zhimo's poetry at any stage of his development.[67] The verses in *Zhimo's Poems* are not crude or immature; they are very lyrical. Xu is notable for this—his poetry has such lyrical qualities that no less than seventeen of his works have been made into songs.[68] Yet they somehow also sound like everyday Chinese speech. The extent to which this is true seems remarkable even today and must have been stunning to those first readers. Cyril Birch (Xu's best critic in English[69]) says that in Xu's poetry "one is struck by the prevalence of natural, everyday phrasing," and that "there (are) no single phrases which (cannot) found in standard modern Chinese usage." Yet, as he points out, "the simplicity is most artfully contrived."[70]

Xu never lapses into writing that is so free that it is no longer poetry, nor does his work ever take on what critics called a "bean-curd block" form, rigidly regular. His response to "the total breakdown of the Chinese poetic tradition," as Birch says, "was endless experimentation with metres and stanzaic forms."[71] Like Chaucer in the 1300s, adapting Italian and French forms to create the first great poetry in vernacular English, or Pushkin in the nineteenth century, steeped in French culture, able to do the same for Russia, the young Chinese poet used "his knowledge of Western poetry"[72] to create a prosody and style that was suited to a "New Poetry" in Chinese. His "experiments and innovations" are still influencing modern poets in China today.[73] Others did work along with him, and even influence him, notably Wen Yiduo, another Crescent Moon poet of great accomplishment. The result of Wen's attempts to find a meter suitable for poetry in modern Chinese is what Cyril Birch calls the *"Dead Water* line,"[74] a meter which was very influential. But Xu never used this meter, or any other one, as a "staple."[75] The endless experimentation mentioned above is the heritage that he left to future Chinese poets, and this, along with the fact that he remained deeply steeped in his own tradition, is what makes him the first great modern Chinese poet. It is no more reasonable to say that Xu was a mere imitator of the British romantic poets (or any other poets) than it would be to call Chaucer Boccaccio lite or a mere imitator of Jean de Meung, or to say that Pushkin's verse is simply Byron Russified, or that he bases his poems entirely on those of Parny.

Xu's accomplishments make translating him difficult, starting with the fact that "normal, everyday Chinese" sounds nothing like normal everyday English. It is not easy to make either sound poetic. Xu often uses literary Chinese stock phrases and combinations but manages to keep sounding conversational in spite of it. He also manages to make foreign structures and styles (usually English) somehow sound natural in his own, very different language.

Let's look at this "conversational" aspect of Xu's poetry a little more deeply. Quite a few of his poems include dialogue.[76] Some of them, in fact, are composed entirely of speech. A *Night In Florence* (p. 124) is a long, dramatic monologue, and *Calvary* (p. 165) is the story of the Crucifixion told in dialogue from the point of view of the crowd, who are common people speaking a slangy, vivid vernacular. But let's discuss one of the short poems, *Bié Níng Wǒ Téng*.

These words, which are both the title and the first line of this piece (p. 99), mean literally, "Don't pinch me, [it] hurts." This is an entirely colloquial Chinese phrase. In the next line, Xu describes the way the woman frowns as she utters it. "You say, and the space between your brows slightly closes." The English translation here does not do justice to the beauty of the Chinese: *nǐ s̲h̲uō, wéi s̲uǒzhe méix̲īn.* It is a seven character line (a number often used in classical poetry), but does not use the tone patterns that were traditionally allowed in seven-syllable regulated verse.[77] Yet it works as poetry, and not just because of the use of sibilants[78] (underlined above) and assonance of the repeated "ei" and "uo" sounds (bolded). The two level tones (second character and final character, marked with a straight line over the words) are not placed as they would be in a classic poem, and you would not be able to use the neutral tone that ends the double character word *suǒzhe* (meaning "close" or "lock") but the line that Xu has written here is lovely when read aloud.

The effects in just that first line, though, go beyond the sound effects. Xu has made a delicate reference to his second wife through the use of the word for "eyebrows," *méi* (眉), which was her name. *Mei* in Chinese is also a synecdoche representing a beautiful woman, one that goes far back into the poetic heritage of several thousand years. This is lovely, but in the next line, Xu does something brilliant. He describes the sound of the word "hurts" (*téng*) describing how it is made in the mouth:

> *Nǎ téng yīgè jīng yuán de bàn tǔ*
> *Zài shéjiān shàng liū zhuǎn*

> That "hurts"—a round essence half spat out
> Turning, sliding on tongue.

Téng, aspirated and plosive, makes a contrast to the sibilants which again predominate in the fourth line and also alliterates with the daring word *tǔ* which means "spit." It's very untraditional to mention spit in a Chinese poem, but it works here. The image of spitting also makes an interesting contrast with "turning and sliding," though these words all describe physical actions.

It is very difficult to get similar sound effects in English, and impossible to retain the allusion. What can be retained is the shift Xu makes at this point from speech into silence and secrets, as the woman's

> Eyes also seem to speak;
> In their brightness ripples rise
> Secrets from the fountain of your heart.

The woman doesn't speak for a few moments at this point, but the imagery remains vivid, not just because it refers to her eyes but because Xu has made his readers feel as if they, too, are looking into those eyes (under those eyebrows). And then the poem moves from the concrete to the intangible, with the single word *meng*, "dreams," which has a line to itself. A brief impressionistic view is given at this point of the place where the poem is situated—the open wine bottle; the mosquito netting over the bed. Then dialogue again, very simple, a question and a response:

> "Are you there—?"
> "Make us die," you say.

And the poem has ended.

In addition to the unorthodox use of words, this poem has a variety of linelengths—of 4, 7, 9, 6, 7, 5, 5, 1, 3, 5, 4, and 6 characters—which would never have been allowed in classical Chinese.[79] It also is punctuated in the modern Western way, with commas, periods, ellipses, and even quotation marks that are alien to traditional Chinese. (I have changed the original punctuation somewhat in my translation.) The poem has no rhyme at the ends of lines, and this is very unclassical, as observed earlier. And yet it works. As always with Xu's poetry, it especially works when it is read aloud.

As in *Don't Pinch, It Hurts*, silence is often important in Xu's poems. The "secrets" that seem to rise from the bottom of the woman's heart in that poem (yet remain unsaid) do not seem to impede the communication between the lovers, but this is not the case in the poem *Late at Night* (p. 103), where Xu uses similar techniques, as he does also in the poem *Coral* (p. 85). In *Late at*

Night the only spoken sentence is "You hurt me—I hate you!" as the couple stands under a corner streetlight. Then we are told that she sobs; but he "doesn't answer." Only the

> Dawn wind gently shakes the tops of the trees.
> Fallen; the early autumn's crimson splendor.

In *Coral* the narrator lets us know in the first stanza that

> You don't need to think I speak
> My heart drowned in the sea's depths long ago
> You don't need to shout at me
> Because I—I can't respond.

Communication is only possible, we are told, if one comes to the place where coral grows under the sea and waits for "the sea wind's fixed moment of silence . . . When you and I can alternately sigh our hidden sighs."

It is not only in his poems about love between a man and a woman that Xu uses this imagery of silence versus speech effectively. Xu wrote many poems about the social problems in China during his life, especially about the suffering of the starving poor, and the callousness of those who had more. In the poem *Mister! Mister!* (p. 68), a young girl begs help from a wealthy man, who is riding "enthroned" in a rickshaw. Most of the poem consists of the child's words. She repeats *xiansheng* (mister) again and again as she asks for some spare change, or for a "bite of steamed bread" to give to her homeless mother, lying ill and frozen by the side of the road. The man only responds once. He says curtly that he didn't bring his money belt.

The main response to the voice of the little girl in the poem is Xu's description of the wheels of the rickshaw. At first, we are told that they are "made of steel," but then, they are "white like ice." Near the end of the poem they are described as "silver" and "shining like silver." One Chinese word for money is silver (just as in English). Finally, the "flying" wheels that "don't stop flying" are "rubber." Rubber wheels are a modern, European innovation that allow the rickshaw to move even faster, to get away from the annoying beggar girl. [80]

Her voice is soon "distant" and all that can be heard by the passenger—and the reader—are those "whirring" wheels.

Objects in Xu's poems often make noises. Sometimes this is onomatopoeia, sometimes simile or metaphor. There is a lot of thunder; loud ocean waves; there are trains, like the one which sounds like oars.[81] Things drop, and break, like the mirror in *Bang!*[82] (p. 103) people cry out, weep—or break suddenly into song. Metaphorical objects can even make sounds. In *Elegy to Mansfield* (p. 163), the wheels of the "imperial carriage"[83] that Hades rides "come shrieking to a halt" near Fontainebleau Palace. But in contrast to the noise, there is often the same silence that there is in response to speech. In his best-known poem, *Cambridge, Farewell Again* (p. 137), this is very marked. "Even the insects are struck dumb, on this summer's evening"—and the poet comes "softly" and leaves "in silence." And in *The Yellow Oriole* (p. 162), the beautiful bird, which is "like spring's brilliance; like passion; like a flame" perches in a tree, in the "dark foliage." The onlookers "passionately hope" that it will sing. It does not. It flies away. "We don't see it again."

Often the poet, the Xu persona, speaks to objects, especially objects in the natural world, and asks them to give him answers. He does this when he is *In Front of Exeter Cathedral* (p. 132). He first asks "the image in front of temple" (most likely a statue of a saint) what the meaning of life is, and then he asks the evening star. The statue does not respond, it is "bewildered"—the star winks at him, in mockery. Finally, he asks an ancient "goitered" tree. For a century, the tree has seen life "in this world" and has seen human beings born and die. It does not answer either. It sighs. Xu sighs in response. That is all.

Sometimes, however, Xu gets answers. Leaves speak to him,[84] the rain whispers as it drains away;[85] the wind speaks to him—the moon often responds. The moon, an image often used in traditional Chinese poetry, is ubiquitous in Xu's poems. It keeps records of the debts of love in a register.[86] It puts on makeup, as night comes.[87] In the fragments of poetry scattered in the essay *Autumn Thoughts on the Indian Ocean*, the moon strokes the ocean with loving silver fingertips and the ocean billows can't prevent themselves from being caressed.

These images are intensely visual; Xu is one of the most visual of poets.

He has what Shakespeare called "the poet's eye."[88] Ironically, in life he was extremely myopic—the large, round-rimmed spectacles Xu was fitted with in childhood have become iconic in China. The poet Bian Zhilin, who was mentored by Xu, told a story about them. According to Bian, when Xu Zhimo put these glasses on and saw the stars for the first time, filling the sky, he was overwhelmed. Perhaps just because he had not always had the ability to see a starry sky—the moon—the ocean—green fields of soybeans or rice, images of things that most of us take for granted (or at least have not looked at carefully) fill his poems. These images are so vivid that one can almost say they are violent. Reading him after reading the classical Chinese poets is like moving one's eyes from the ink-brush painting *Early Spring*[89] to a vivid work by Delacroix. Xu's whites, blacks, golds, and bright reds jump off the page, often juxtaposed and in contrast to each other, and it is not only the color in the poems that give the reader the sense of sudden sight. He is a master of metaphor. His grain lies in rows "like striped silk"; his sun sets "like a stowaway" or else has a face like "red decay"; under the water, his plants "swagger"; blood lies on snow after a massacre like the petals of plum flowers; clouds "seize" the sky or else "attack" it. This is very powerful—and not traditionally Chinese. But as with the paintings of Delacroix, traditional culture has not vanished from the poems of Xu Zhimo. Those are not the sleeves of a European shirt that Xu is shaking out as he bids farewell to Cambridge, so capacious that they could hold "the clouds in your Western sky." One remembers that Xu's preferred garb was a Chinese *changpao* worn over his pair of European style trousers, a comfortable blending of two cultures. Ma Xuecong says that not just Xu, but the whole Crescent Moon group were "conservatives."

The meeting and blending of the old and new in Xu—the native and the foreign—has been much studied since his poems have been resurrected, though. And the Communists' former claim that he merely imitated "decadent" Western styles has been put definitively to rest. Serious study has shown that Xu created what I like to call "a lyric fusion"—West and East, including the "east" of Tagore. It is now acknowledged that his work is highly original.

Xu the Romantic

There is another stereotype of Xu that needs to be addressed in any introduction to his poetry, though. This is the image of Xu the "romantic," a term with several meanings, of course—some of them intertwined. As a philosophy, it implies an idealistic view of life; a visionary view, which may or may not be justified. A romantic probably also has a strong affinity for the beauties of nature. Someone who believes in the transforming power of love between a man and woman is also a romantic, especially if the person is seeking a love which will take them out of mundane, everyday existence into a "higher" plane. Then there is Romanticism in the arts, "characterized by an emphasis on subjective emotional qualities and freedom of form."[90] This is thought of as an outmoded style, replaced by modernism when the nineteenth century gave way to the twentieth. Whether this means that poets who continued to write in the older style, by their own choice, are inferior to the more "modern" ones, however, is a contested point. Michelle Yeh defends Xu for writing poems in the Romantic style, stating that "The dismissal of romanticism is underscored by an evolutionist view of literary history that romanticism is outdated and obsolete as a vibrant influence on contemporary poetry since it has been replaced by modernism and other trends."[91] She thinks this view is wrong.

23

Was Xu really a Romantic, though? He was certainly an idealist; he certainly also celebrated the beauties of nature, and that he believed love could be a transforming force is something that no one who has read his poems can deny—nor anyone who considers his life choices. He has, though, a considerable body of work which shows "a surprising depth of gloom"[92] as Cyril Birch points out. This surprises Birch because he thinks it does not fit with the overwhelming evidence from Xu's friends and contemporaries about his cheerful and ebullient personality. Attempting to square this evidence with the mournful poems, Birch went so far as to say that the only real Xu is the poet in his *allegro* (happy) moods and that he is imitating Thomas Hardy, one of his role models, when he becomes *penseroso* (brooding).[93] Birch was especially anxious to do this because the Marxist critics, analyzing the poems, attributed

Xu's "moods of failure and pessimism" and what they call his "increasing timidity" to "the decline of the whole bourgeois literary movement."[94]

This is obvious nonsense. Birch, however, is cherry-picking the evidence also, when he states that Xu's friends and contemporaries all describe him as perpetually joyful. Xu did have "carefree, youthful exuberance" as his "hallmark" but "he could be suddenly melancholy . . . When he was moody, the sky would fall and the earth splinter."[95] This is not something that came upon him in his last years, either (one reason the "class-consciousness" theory does not hold water). In 1924, Xu gave a speech called *Fallen Leaves* (p. 193) at Peking University. He wrote an essay based on this, describing melancholy as a

> . . . strange thing, shifting, shapeless—something that you cannot clearly describe. When it comes to a person, their whole body feels trapped, as if caught in a spider's web. If you struggle, you can move, say, stretch an arm out, but you cannot become unstuck. It is a very frightening web.

Xu said he "knew it well." He added that he also knew "what listlessness is like. Its eyes and its disgusting countenance." Even earlier, in 1923, he wrote the poem *Sadness* (p. 129). This contains another devastating portrait of depression, depression so heavy that the sufferer feels

> My heart like an ancient mound
> Covered with rootless weeds
> My heart like a frozen spring
> Ice blocking up the living fountain
> My heart like an insect when winter comes
> In hibernation—its mouth stopped—

This is clearly based on personal experience. Xu did not need Thomas Hardy to show him what misery is like. He did not need the nineteenth-century Romantic poets, either. They, of course, also fell into "deep gloom" as often as they showed transports of joy in their poetry—both sadness and happiness being "subjective emotions." They were delighted to go into detail, and at length, with their individualistic descriptions of any feelings, something that is not common in traditional Chinese poetry. There is some shadow of this in Chinese literature—one thinks of Lin Daiyu burying the flowers in the classic novel *Dream of the Red Chamber* (*Hong Lou Meng*)—but even that seems somehow abstracted to a more general sadness about transience and mortality, less personal than described in Shelley's *Ode to a Skylark*:

> We look before and after,
> And pine for what is not:
> Our sincerest laughter
> With some pain is fraught;
> Our sweetest songs are those that tell of saddest thought.

Shelley speaks of laughter in the lines above, but Xu differs, in my opinion, from the both Shelley and Keats in the way that laughter in his poems is often aimed at himself. He is ironical in a way that they are not, "self-conscious" in the sense that the majority of the time he seems to distance himself slightly from his emotions, so that he is aware enough of them to mock them when it seems that he is danger of going too far.

This is already true in Xu's earliest poetic efforts. In *Dewdrops on Grass*, previously discussed as Xu's blueprint delineating the role of a poet-sage, there is ironic laughter. Before Xu describes the ideal, he addresses what he feels is the reality and speaks to a "poet" (possibly himself) whose "fountains of creativity" are stopped up. In the fourth line of the second stanza, Xu transcribes the sound of a derisive snicker. The Chinese character used and repeated is *chi* (嗤).[96] I have translated this as "Ha! Ha!" but the Chinese definitely implies mockery in a way that the English does not.

"Ha! Ha!" Xu says, and then describes in some spectacularly lyrical lines how the mountains create jade, the sea makes pearls, and how the heavens make music,[97] while the poet—addressed familiarly with the word *yo* (哟), meaning something like "hey you"—is silenced; dumb; impotent. He not only can't create—he can't even gather up what is being freely offered, throughout the poem, by all of nature, what he is told to "receive, receive."[98] This fact is so vividly expressed—the fact of the poet's impotence and ineptness—that it stays in the reader's mind even after the poem segues into the elevated, ringing description of how the sage and seer ought to stand "above the clouds and birds . . . on the summit of fully lived life."[99] Xu seems to fear that he is none of these things—yet. This undercuts the elevated message of the whole poem. Yet it also is what makes the poem work a great deal better than *Sunrise on Mount Tai*. The latter poem tells us about Xu's admiration for Tagore, something that it is very important to know, but all the elevated statements, the tangled metaphors, the constant exhortations to "sing!" "praise!"—even the overuse of exclamation marks (typical of Xu in this sort of mood)—all of this is a bit exhausting to read. One is grateful that Xu's poetry is not often like this. One is grateful that usually, even when he is very serious, he cannot help the ironic touch.

Xu deals with the theme of sadness often in his poems. In *Sadness* (p. 129), Xu is very structured. He asks rhetorically if "sadness" is in various spots around the place where he is writing. He starts with the sky above him, and then turns to the courtyard he is in, continuing to come physically closer to himself as he questions, asking about his brush, his paper and—finally—his heart. When he asks if sadness is in the sky, and then replies that it is not, he uses imagery appropriate for the heavens:

> Blue and long, white and vast
> Clouds and birds returning, dancing;
> Cosmos of bright air . . .

By the time he comes to ask the same question concerning the paper he is writing on, he lets us know personal things about himself. The paper has, he tells us, "sentimental feelings and sexual desire" though it is "in its essence, pure." But sadness is not in it. Then the fact that he is being ironical becomes clear as he describes his heart in a devastating series of metaphors in which he compares it to a mount covered with weeds, a frozen spring, a mute insect—and one realizes that he is so sad that his whole environment is imbued with his grief. At this point, the poem segues into a strict meter that counterbalances the strong emotion. And then he ends the poem with irony, not humorous, but sarcastic. The sarcasm saves the poem from self-pity. "No! Sadness is not in my heart."

Xu uses humor in the first of many, many poems about his tears in *Little Poem* (p. 84), when he asks if he has paid his "debt of tears," mentioned earlier. The fact that Xu asks "is this a new account, or have I paid my debt?" makes the reader feel that, while he's unhappy, he also notes the absurdity of the situation. So while Xu weeps "hot and cold tears" (and will continue weeping, as will the lovers in his poems) his emotionalism, distanced as it is, does not become too tiresome to us.

If Xu used irony to present his emotions to his readers and to invite them to participate in those emotions, without overwhelming them and falling into bathos, he also used it when he wrote his poems about China's weighty problems. As we have seen, he was deeply grieved by these, and wrote about them often. He not only would not identify himself with a political party, though; he also would not write polemic. Irony helped him to avoid that.

An example of this is *On Leaving Japan* (p. 64), written in 1924.[100] In its beginning stanzas, Xu sets up a strong contrast between China and Japan, which seems to be in Japan's favor; however, the reader soon realizes that it is not. Obliquely (and very beautifully) Xu begins to refer to China's past glory, although also (very honestly) to her flaws. The control shown in the poem is extreme—partly a matter of control of form (strict meter, strict rhyme, carefully placed repetition) and partly control over the words he allows himself to use.

Xu leaves direct comparison behind though in the poem *Cricket* (p. 74), written in 1927. He reverts again to subdued irony. The poem begins with an address to an insect, "Cricket, why are you here?" and ends with the "Soul" addressing Xu (and the readers) prophesying "Revolution." Xu speaks to the cricket, which is close by because in the old China these insects were pets, kept in cages, not so much because they sing but rather because they were fighters and there was betting on cricket matches. The kind of leisure that allowed this is no more. Xu is distressed by what has replaced it. Poetry is useless, love is not valued, materialism is rampant, integrity is gone, and people with various political philosophies battle each other. (These are the "isms" which "rape thought.") These battles had actually already become physical battles, civil war—they were not just polemical. Human life had become cheap, as the warlords, Communists, and KMT competed for power and all committed atrocities.[101] Xu personifies all of this in the poem, and this allows him to keep a certain distance from what he is saying—and thus does not seem to preach or rail. Again, the structure of the poem helps with this. Xu stays within a prescribed number of syllables and uses strictly rhyming couplets.[102] He also uses another strategy to draw the reader in, the same one that we saw in the much less serious earlier poems, that of a gentle self-criticism—or at least an awareness and admission of his flaws. Society is in such a state, he says, that he simply wants to withdraw—his soul wants to "stay in a garden and plant"—a statement which, to a Chinese reader, would evoke not Voltaire but the ancient scholar-officials who became recluses when the times were out of joint. He wants to keep his distance, while others make "pigs, dogs, worms" of themselves and ultimately "fall." But this distance is not the answer. It will cause *rendao*—"charity" or "benevolence," to wither and die. And revolution is the inevitable result of decent people's withdrawal. (China had of course already had one revolution, in 1911, and it had not been pleasant, nor had it had, thus far, good results.)

Withdrawal

The ultimate withdrawal is, of course, death. Xu is often suspected of having desired this because of some of the lines and sections in his poems, especially *qing si* (情死), the "love-death," which he appears to be glorifying in poems such as *A Night in Florence*. Love-death does not come from Wagner; it is also an old, old Chinese idea. In Chinese literature, it generally is not a matter of two lovers committing suicide, either together or separately, because of truly bad circumstances (Antony and Cleopatra) or a fateful series of misunderstandings (Romeo and Juliet). In traditional China, true lovers also did not need knives or poison. They can simply die from unhappiness, like Lin Dai Yu (consumption helps her along)[103] or like Zhu Ying-tai and Liang Shanbo, the "Butterfly Lovers."

Xu found this idea attractive, certainly, whether in Western or Eastern form. He translated sections of *Romeo and Juliet*; he raved admiringly about Wagner, writing a poem about his music and an essay about the man, just as he had about Mansfield, Hardy, and Tagore; and the lovers in his own poems do often say "let's die" as they fantasize about being together forever and escaping "it all." "All" included traditional mores, traditional parents, spouses chosen in arranged marriages, and every unpleasant obstacle that prevented soulmates, two people who had chosen each other freely, from passionately becoming one. We saw how this did not work out as Xu wished in his own life, but he wrote poetry with this theme until the end. His last great poem, *Love's Inspiration*, is the supreme example. In this poem the heroine dies—her monologue is given on her death bed. She does not kill herself and she does not die because of love—the fact that she is dying allows her to honestly reveal her love; that is all. The prose poem that he literally titles "love-death" (translated *Liebestod*, p. 122) is actually about roses being picked. The roses die. The person who plucks them is bloodied by the thorns of the flowers he or she is gathering (and killing) and there is a lot of symbolism, but no real "ending it all" in this poem. The woman speaking in *A Night in Florence* says it would be lovely to die because of love, and then wafts into a fantasy in which she sees her own dead body in her lover's arms. Her lover, who is leaving the next day, does not answer her. When she does finally suggest "let's die together," her lover (whose voice is never heard in the poem) clearly refuses. She then delivers the pragmatic (and funny) line "Well, I can't die then; a love-death takes two or it's not a love-death."

So, like the majority of Xu's lovers, these live. The man leaves the next day, one presumes, as planned. The world goes on. Even though *This is A Coward's World* (p. 102), people don't leave it so easily either to die, or to escape to that far island across the "wide, wide white sea," the island which is "heaven." Xu knows this. His head may be in the clouds, he may admire the beauty that "can't be stopped or delayed" as it sets out on a *Cloud Voyage* (p. 158)—he may even want to be a cloud but his feet remain on the ground. He will always refuse the *White-Whiskered Old Man of the Sea* (p. 86), "playing his odd tricks on me"—and although he fears the next grappling with this creature, this fact merely maintains an interesting tension in his poetry. Xu's people are more likely to die for art than for love—as the singer in *Sea Rhyme* (p. 160) does. Few of the poems tilt over into pure, unthinking emotion. Xu is too great a poet—and technician—to succumb to that.

So, although I would agree that Xu's leanings were Romantic and that many of his greatest poems (like the *Cambridge Farewell*) are in a style that is not just romantic but seems nostalgic, if not old-fashioned, to a Western reader, there is more to him than that. There are poems like *Unexpected* (p. 148). This rhymeless poem, based almost on the form of a limerick, is not in a nineteenth-century style (though it is based on the sentiments familiar to the Romantics). What about *Broad Sea and Empty Sky?*

30

> Broad sea and empty sky I have no need of.
> And I have no wish to release a huge paper hawk
> To fly up to heaven and harass the winds in all directions—
> > I just want a minute
> > I just want a flash of light
> > I just want a crevice that's tight;
> Like a child climbing up to a window sill
> In a dark room lying in wait there and
> Gazing up at the sky to the west and the undying cre-
> vice, light-
> flash, mi-
> nute.

This poem is not only very unromantic in its content, but it is a concrete poem, with the sentiments in it mirrored by its kite form as it dwindles from the "broad" first line, to the last little syllable—an effect that is even more marked when it is written in ideographs. It is the opposite of "I want to fly," as the poet constricts himself, leaving nature for a dark corner and constricted space. The space is one from which he can see a "light-flash," however. And the poem is considered to be among Xu's finest.

Xu left many masterpieces, however. And he left more than that. Stylistically, he left a treasure trove for the poets who are his heirs, up to contemporary times, as his many varied styles and his metrical experimentation showcase so many of the possibilities for Chinese vernacular verse. He left, like Tagore, songs that everybody sings in his native land. And he left something very important to the whole world. I spoke at the beginning of the essay about the Red Guards. Xu died; he was pinned down under a monument, just as Madame Bai, the white snake who is often an image in his poems was pinned down under Thunder Peak Pagoda.[104] The Red Guards ripped the stone up and attempted to obliterate his memory, scattering his remains. This was not meaningless savagery. Even dead, Xu Zhimo was a threat. His vision of the world lived on and stood against their narrow, polemical vision—his idealistic, broad ideas about freedom and beauty in different places and cultures and his certainty that people from the East and the West *can* connect. Now that the Guards have vanished, that vision still lives on, the vision of a poet-seer, a poet-prophet. It has Chinese flocking in their millions to Cambridge—and my hope is that these translations of his work will help English readers to understand his vision and to share it.

Repaired tombstone of Xu Zhimo in Xiashi, Zhejiang.

NOTES

1   Hsu Kai-yu, in "Hsu Chih-mo," *Twentieth Century Chinese Poetry: An Anthology* (Anchor Books, 1964), pp. 76–77.

2   Jonathan Spence, *The Gate of Heavenly Peace: The Chinese and Their Revolution 1895–1980* (Penguin Books, 1982), p. 275.

3   Liu Yan Sheng, *Xu Zhimo's Biography* (Jinan University Press, 1996), p. 1.

4   Tony S. Hsu, *Chasing the Modern* (Cam Rivers Publishing, 2017), p. 100.

5   A web search of "Xuzhimo Cambridge" or "Xu Zhimo YouTube" will bring up numerous articles and videos about the memorial stone and garden, and the phenomenon of Chinese tourism there.

6   I have translated this title (再別康橋) as *Cambridge, Farewell Again*, since the Chinese does not say that it is the "second" farewell, rather that he is saying goodbye "again."

7   Xu Zhimo is the Pinyin rendering of the poet's name (徐志摩); for those unfamiliar with this romanization system, Shu Jer-mow would be an approximation of how the name sounds in standard Mandarin. In the Wade-Giles system of romanization, it is spelled Hsu Chih-mo and one still sees this rendering. Xu himself wrote his name in Roman letters as Tsemou Hsu, reflecting the way he would have pronounced it, as a native of Zhejiang where the Mandarin pronunciation differs slightly (roughly, Shu **Tser**-mow).

8   In the Chinese lunar calendar, years start at different times than do Western years, and thus there has been confusion about the date of Xu Zhimo's birth in Western sources. He was born on January 15 by our dating, in the 22nd year of the Guangxu emperor. That year ran from February 13, 1896, to February 2, 1897, so Xu was born in 1897.

9   Since the Opium War in 1839.

10   Also called the New Culture Movement. May Fourth would come to describe the political side and New Culture the cultural and literary side.

11   Jonathan Spence, in *The Gate of Heavenly Peace* (Penguin, 1982) describes many of these students.

12   John C. H. Wu, *Beyond East and West* (Sheed and Ward, 1951), p. 65–66, describes how they chose their English names.

13 Gaylord Kai-Loh Leung, *Hsu Chih-mo, A Literary Biography* (PhD diss., SOAS, University of London, 1972), p. 13. This name may also mean, "The monk (named) Zhi touched me." One can understand this in English as something like the 'laying on of hands' in some religious traditions.

14 Natasha Pang-Mei Chang, *Bound Feet and Western Dress* (Bantam, 1996), pp. 68–9. See Tony S. Hsu, *Chasing the Modern,* for further information about the Zhang (Chang) family.

15 Gaylord Leung discusses this best in his *Hsu Chih-mo, A Literary Biography*, pp. 17–20.

16 *Chasing the Modern*, pp. 32–33.

17 Ibid, p. 20.

18 Michelle Yeh, *Modern Chinese Poetry: Theory and Practice Since 1917* (Yale University Press, 1991).

19 Ibid, p. 13 quoting Ping-ti Ho, *The Ladder of Success in Imperial China: Aspects of Social Mobility.*

20 Ibid.

21 八不 translated in Yeh, Modern Chinese Poetry, p. 11.

22 *Dewdrops on Grass*, p. 41, seems to have survived by accident, and was not published until 1980 according to Liang Ren in *The Complete Poems of Xu Zhimo*, who states that the original handwritten manuscript is dated November 23, 1921 (*Xu Zhimo Shi Quan Bian*, ed. Liang Ren, Zhejiang Artistic Press, 1990, p. 6).

23 Cyril Birch has beautifully translated a great deal of Xu's essay, *The Cambridge I Knew,* (我所知道的康橋) in *Anthology of Chinese Literature, Volume 2: From the 14ᵗʰ Century to the Present Day,* ed. Cyril Birch (Grove Press, 1972), pp. 341–47.

24 Spence, *Heavenly Peace,* p. 275; the unknown high school student memorializing Xu calls him "Our poet-sage." See also Pearl S. Buck, *My Several Worlds* (Pocket Books, 1956), p. 198.

25 Leo Ou-fan Lee, *The Romantic Generation of Modern Chinese Writers* (Harvard University Press, 1973), p. 166.

26 Mansfield was a short story writer who wrote only a few poems, but the analogy still applies. Xu translated more of her writing than he did of anyone else and almost single-handedly made her one of the most admired writers in China, a role model to this day.

27 Michelle Yeh, ed., *Anthology of Modern Chinese Poetry* (Yale University Press, 1992), p. 9.

28 Cyril Birch, "Hsu Chih-mo's Debt to Thomas Hardy," in *Tamkang Review,* vol. 8, no. 1, 1977, pp. 1–24.

29 Hsu, *Chasing the Modern*, pp. 38–41.

30 Ibid, p. 40.

31 Lee, *The Romantic Generation of Modern Chinese Writers,* p. 170.

32 Buck, *My Several Worlds,* p. 198. Lin Yutang leaves another portrait of Xu by a contemporary in his novel, *Moment in Peking* (John Day, 1939). He names the Xu persona "Paku" and tells readers that he "dominated every circle in which he appeared . . . He seemed to breathe a spirit of youth and amiability wherever he went" (p. 513). A few pages later Lin describes the poet's "white and noble face" (p. 515). The truly interesting thing is that, while they both knew him well, both Lin and Buck wrote these remarks years after Xu's death. He was attractive, it seems, in a way that was memorable.

33 Hsu, *Chasing the Modern,* p. 40.

34 Lee, *The Romantic Generation of Modern Chinese Writers,* p. 159, quoting Hu Shi.

35 Divorce was actually not common even among the "advanced" thinkers with whom Xu spent his time. Xu's heroes Percy Bysshe Shelley, Bertrand Russell, and Katherine Mansfield had all divorced, but paid a high social price.

36 It is interesting to compare John Wu's description of his happy arranged marriage on p. 61 of his autobiography, *Beyond East and West*, with Xu's divorce experience. Wu, a close long-time friend, was one of the go-betweens Xu sent to Zhang Youyi to arrange the divorce. Chang, *Bound Feet,* pp. 140, 142.

37 Chang, *Bound Feet,* p. 141.

38 Also known as Phyllis Lin.

39 See Wilma Fairbank, *Liang and Lin: Partners in Exploring China's Architectural Past* (University of Pennsylvania Press, 2008) for the story of their marriage and their achievements as the first Western-trained architects in China.

40 If she ever was his. How much Xu and Lin were romantically involved is something that is rather endlessly debated in China. That they were lifelong friends, however, is not in doubt.

41 In traditional China, the seduction of a married woman, or even enticing her to leave her husband, could result in both the wife and the seducer being sentenced to death by torture.

42 Liang Qichao famously gave the couple a public scolding during the actual ceremony.

43 Zhang Youyi told her side of the story to her great-niece, Natasha Pang-mei Chang, who published it in 1997 in *Bound Feet and Western Dress.* Lu Xiaoman published her diaries after Xu's death. Lin Huiyin was an important twentieth-century poet and writer and is considered a member of the Crescent Moon Society, although membership in that group is complicated. See Ma Xuecong, *The Crescent Moon School: The Poets, Poetry, and Poetics of a Modern Conservative Intellectual Group in Republican China* (PhD diss., University of Edinburgh, 2017).

44 www.nobelprize.org/prizes/literature/1913/summary/

45 Kripalana, Krishna *Rabindranath Tagore, A Biography* (Grove Press), 1962, p. 311ff.

46 Gitanjali actually means "Song Offering."

47 He had renounced the knighthood that he had received from George V in 1919 to protest the Jallianwallah Bagh Massacre, among other acts at this time.

48 This was in addition to the foundation of Santiniketan.

49 Spence, *Heavenly Peace*, p. 213, quoting Stephen Hay from *Asian Ideas of East and West: Tagore and His Critics in Japan, India and China* (Cambridge, MA, 1970).

50 Soymié, Michel, "China: The Struggle for Power," *Larousse World Mythology*, ed. Pierre Grimal (Excalibur Books, 1981), p. 174.

51 *Sunrise on Mount Tai*, p. 176.

52 Spence, *Heavenly Peace*, p. 213, quoting Hay, *Asian Ideas of East and West.*

53 www.taiwantoday.tw/news.php?post=26294&unit=20,29,35,45

54 Spence, *Heavenly Peace,* p. 216, again quoting Hay.

55 https://taiwantoday.tw/news.php?post=26294&unit=20,29,35,45

56 Lee, *Romantic Generation,* p. 146.

57 新月派

58 Tagore, Rabindranath, *The Crescent Moon,* 1913.

59 For a discussion of this group, its significance and its members at different times, see Ma Xuecong, *The Crescent Moon School,* op. cit.

60 Ma Xuecong, *Crescent Moon,* pp. 51–59.

61 Lin, Julia C., *Modern Chinese Poetry, An Introduction* (University of Washington Press, 1973), p. 3.

62 In Xu's time, one consulted rhyming dictionaries to figure this out.

63 According to the type of poem. See Lin, *Modern Chinese Poetry,* pp. 3–17 for a more detailed explanation of the mechanics of classical Chinese poetry. James C.Y. Liu's monograph *The Art of Chinese Poetry* gives the best explanation of this subject available in English, in my opinion, though.

64 Yeh, *Modern Chinese Poetry*, p. 22.

65 Quoted in Yeh, ibid.

66 Lin, *Modern Chinese Poetry,* p. 3.

67 See Birch, *English and Chinese Metres in Hsu Chih-mo,* p. 290 for Yu Ping-bo's assessment of Xu's stages of development, written in 1931. Although this is a useful assessment in many ways, I do not agree with Birch and Yu that Xu's poetry showed any "steady chronological development" but with Ma Xuecong who shows that not just Xu, but all the Crescent poets wrote many different sorts of poetry at all periods.

68 Yeh, Michelle, "Xu Zhimo, The Quintessential Modern Poet," in Hsu, Tony S., *Chasing the Modern,* pp. 114–115.

69 Birch, Cyril, "English and Chinese Metres in Hsu Chih-mo," Institute of History and Philology of the Academia Sinica, vol. 8, 1960, pp. 258–93. Birch analyzes the metrical patterns of two poems by Xu, *Dead leaves* and *A Song of the Sea.*

70 Ibid, p 268. This essay is well worth reading for a better understanding of Xu even though I (and others) do not agree with the way in which Birch analyzes what he calls Chinese "metre."

71 Birch, *Hsu Chih-mo's Debt to Thomas Hardy,* p. 8.

72 Lin, *Modern Chinese Poetry,* p. 102.

73 Ibid.

74 After the title of Wen's most famous poem. Birch discusses this in depth in *English and Chinese Metres,* p. 279. The discussion is brilliant, but highly technical.

75 Ibid.

76 Browning's influence is obvious.

77 Lin, *Modern Chinese Poetry,* p. 7, has a a succinct description of what is allowable.

78 The letter"x" has a sound like "sh" in the Pinyin romanization of Chinese.

79 Except if it were a *ci* set to an ancient tune with the line lengths mapped out to match the lost music.

80 The rickshaw itself was a modern invention and the vulcanized wheels an innovation in the 1920s when Xu was writing. See Strand, David, *Rickshaw Beijing: City People and Politics in the 1920s* (University of California Press, 1989).

81 See *On the Shanghai-Hangzhou line*, p. 47.

82 The onomatopoeic *DingDang* is part of the Chinese title, but I made a rare change as that sounds too much like DingDong in English.

83 I translated this as "car of state."

84 See *Bang!,* p. 103.

85 See *Whispers,* p. 106.

86 See *Little Poem,* p 84. Keeping this register is the job of the Goddess of Disillusionment in the greatest Chinese novel, *The Dream of the Read Chamber (Hong Lou Meng) by Cao Xueqin* (1715 or 1724–1763 or 1764), aka *The Story of the Stone (Shitou Ji)* in David Hawke's translation.

87 See *Toward Evening*, p. 50.

88 *Midsummer Night's Dream*, Act 5, scene 1.

89 早春圖, a painting by Guo Xi (1020–90), is one of the greatest masterpieces of Song landscape painting.

90 *Merriam-Webster Dictionary* https://www.merriam-webster.com/dictionary/romantic

91 Yeh's essay, in Hsu, *Chasing the Modern*, p. 117.

92 Birch, "Hsu Chih-mo's Debt to Thomas Hardy," p. 15.

93 Ibid, p. 17. The reference is to John Milton's two poems with those Italian titles.

94 Ibid, pp. 15–16.

95 Lee, Leo Oufan, *Romantic Generation*, p. 149. He quotes Xu's friend, Lin Yutang.

96 Stanza 2, line 1 and repeated throughout the poem.

97 Lines 4–7.

98 Stanza 4, line 9.

99 Stanzas 5–9.

100 After his visit to China, Tagore continued on to Japan, and was accompanied by Xu.

101 See *Plum Blossom and Snow Compete for Spring*, p. 70.

102 I was not able to replicate the rhyme in my translation.

103 Interestingly, Xu's great love, Lin Hui Yin, who had a lot in common with the "talented beauty" Lin Dai Yu, did ultimately succumb to tuberculosis. She did not die for the love of Xu, however—if anything other than lung disease hastened her death, it was the attacks against her and her husband for being intellectuals in Mao's China. See more on Lin and Xu in the commentary beginning on p. 110.

104 Bonett, Dorothy Trench, *Repairing the Sky*, 2018, p. 98–110.

23. XI. 21

草上的露珠儿
    颗颗是透明的水晶球,
新归来的蜂儿
    在花里忙个不休,

诗人呵! 可不是春光吟
    还在开放你
    创造的诗泉,
尝呵! 吐不尽南山北山
        的璠瑜

Manuscript of Dewdrops on Grass, dated November 23, 1921.

THE
EARLIEST
POEM

Dewdrops on Grass

草上的露珠儿

Dewdrops on grass
Each one a limpid crystal ball;
Swallows returned to their old nests,
Each murmuring, without a lull—

Ah, poet! How can this be?
Spring coming to our midst has not released
The fountain of your creativity—
Ha! Ha! The mountains can't stop spitting jade.
The oceans, west and east, unceasingly sprinkle pearls;
Harmonious like rhyme, flute, pipe and zither fuse
And drink and eat the radiance of stars, sun, moon!
Ah, poet! How can this be?
Spring coming to our midst has not released
The fountain of your creativity—

The voice of thunder

Shatters a sky filled with fog

The sun ascends to shine with brilliance

Rises again to face its golden throne;

Soft wind from the south

Wrinkles the ardent face of the sea as it blows

And gulls rise, white and clean, to pierce the clouds

Then fall back at their ease into the waves, where they roam;

Ah, poet! It's time to board the fishing boat

How is it that you aren't prepared yet

To recite, to sing?

Ah, look! In that white wave

Golden-winged sea carp,

White, tender salamander

Shrimp barbels; crab bellies.

Ah, quick! A net set out, a fish hook put out—

Receive! Receive!

Your parents, wife, son, relatives, friends

Surely will enjoy these rare delicacies, these priceless treasures.

Ah, poet! It's time to board the fishing boat

how is it that you aren't prepared yet

To recite, to sing?

Ah, poet!

It's you! the one who must be first to sense the spirit of the age.

It's you! the one who must integrate action and thought.

It's you! the one who must forge the boundary between man and heaven—

Your riches—rivers seas winds clouds

Birds beasts flowers grass gods ghosts mosquitoes flies—

A word from you hides them; in heaven's alphabet earth's alphabet human

writing—

Your vast furnace: Imagination;

Your flame burning forever: Inspiration;

Forging poems, changing beauty, changing splendor greatness—

You stand tall, tall above meadow lark skylark—

Stretching across the four seas, not asking about past ages or modern times—

Spreading a rare splendor of music—

It's you! the philanthropist who knows the essence of poverty's source;

It's you! displaying the benevolence and beauty a rainbow has—

It's you! you reside on the highest peak of fully lived life!

43

[HANDWRITTEN DRAFT DATED] NOVEMBER 23, 1921

This first poem of Xu's that has been preserved (with the exception of a tra-
ditional poem published in a school newspaper in 1914) is discussed in detail
beginning on p. 6 of the Introduction. It was not published until 1980 in
Taiwan, but has since become widely known. Xu may not have published it
because he considered it to be from what he called his "apprenticeship," which
may be a little misleading, as his entire poetic career lasted barely nine years
(1922 to 1931).

Vignettes
(Brush Sketches)

Spotted Cow Song

花牛歌

The spotted cow, in the grass, sits.
Flattened, cut grain looks like stripes on silk—

The spotted cow, in the grass, dozes.
And the white clouds seize, fiercely, half the sky—

The spotted cow, in the grass, walks.
Its swishing tail like water murmuring—*liu, liu*—

The spotted cow, in the grass, dreams;
While like a stowaway behind blue, west peaks, sun sets.

[1923]

The Sun in August
八月的太阳

The sun in August yellows as it dries.
Who says that this world is not made of gold?
The sparrows doze in the shade of the trees
And children in the grass tumble and roll;

The sun in August yellows as it dries.
Who says that this world is not made of gold?
Of golden woods and also golden lawns,
And of sparrows that happily make noises;
And golden chestnuts heaped in golden hoards,
While golden are the peasants' laughing voices.

[1923]

These two poems were first published in 1937. The drafts (in the possession of Wang Tongzhao, a friend of Xu Zhimo) are believed to be from around 1923, but are undated.

Wild Geese

雁儿们

Wild geese fly in the clouds
    Look at their wings
    Look at their wings
Sometimes they return
    Sometimes they rush.

Wild geese fly in the clouds
    Evening clouds color their bodies
    Evening clouds color their bodies
Sometimes as bright as silver
    Sometimes with golden rays.

Wild geese fly in the clouds
    Listen to their song
    Listen to their song
Sometimes they lament
    Sometimes freely rejoice.

Wild geese fly in the clouds
    Why do they soar?
    Why do they soar?
Do they miss their companions?
Do they have no ancestral homes?

Wild geese fly in the clouds
    Dusk will soon make the world dark
    Dusk will soon make the world dark
Their journey forward will not be in light
    Where will their young fly?

The world sleeps peacefully in darkness
    Dusk veils the mountain forests
    Dusk urges the sea to sleep
And who is there to hear now
    The lament rising in the dark?

[1931]

On the Shanghai-Hangzhou Line

沪杭车中

Fast fast fast! Rush rush rush!
Cloud dots—mountain slice—curl of smoke—
And whoosh! A noise like oars—bridge—over water—
Pine forest—bamboos—red leaves whirl—fall—

Sumptuous autumn! Sumptuous fields—woods—
Distinct as in a dream; blurring; dissolved—
Fast! Fast! Train wheels turn? Or . . . Time?
Autumn scenery rushes by—Life rushes on—

[1923]

Awake!

醒!醒!

Spring brightness—peaceful—
Fills the duck pond.
Quick! Bid your lonely dreams goodbye
Come pluck begonias, play in the pond.

[UNDATED FRAGMENT, FIRST
PUBLISHED IN 1983]

Midnight: Wind in the Pines

夜半松风

This is a mountain slope, a winter night;
Beneath the slope, a desolate monk's hut—
Inside the hut, a dreaming, lonely soul,
Praying, repenting, sinking in lost hopes—

Bawling out loud and howling—why?
Like drum like gong like tiger leopard howl—
Seeking in secret and confessing—why?
O—tragedy of love—O—life so cruel—
Until again the flood, the tide submerging—
The frenzied dreamer in his lonely hut.

[1922]

Wildflower in the Morning Fog

朝雾里的小草花

Unexpected! Wildflower; exquisite and small.
Your bright, pearlescent shining
Like the gleam of a moth.
In the darkness, you long for
The flaming colors of the evening clouds;

While in the grass thicket, across the road
In the midst of desolation, despair, astonishment,
Under a stone wall, disoriented in this fog
I meditate on human life, and evanescent dew—
And my tears fall.

[1924]

This is the first of two poems titled *Two Little Poems about Mt. Lu* (庐山小诗
两首).

Toward Evening

向晚

I can't help but praise
This April day as it draws toward evening,
Embracing clouds and embracing the trees,
And the jade-like delicacy of rice fields.

The clouds lay siege now to the limpid sky
White like swallows from the immortal isles;
Rose sunset clouds shine on them; they are like
Feathers embroidering the gold-edged sky.

And oxen, their work done, dreaming mute dreams
In the evening, walk quick down hidden paths;
The children who herd them crouch by their sides
Wanting to climb their backs and vault upon them.

And in the shade of the circumspect trees
A white stone bridge straddles a flowing stream;
Black night comes, swift, to fill this bridge's eaves—
While stars flash, tumbling, in the waves beneath.

The soy fields—green. Hidden, the mulberry trees.
Sad seems the thicket by the mountain stream.
But tranquil are the evening fields and scenes,
Though—listen! in the grass the insects scream!

And see! The moon putting her makeup on
In the twilight, while the panicked sun
Flees skyward, fearing she'll see him and mock
The red ruin that his face has become!

[UNDATED]

Movie: Thunder Peak Pagoda Under the Moon

月下雷峰影片

I send you the shadow of Thunder Peak Pagoda;
Whole sky dense with black clouds, white clouds—
I send you the summit of Thunder Peak Pagoda
Bright moon pouring shadow on sleeping, beating heart.

Deep, deep black night; tower shadow leaning, leaning—
Round, round colored moon, reflections in water gleaming—
If you and I row a small skiff without a roof to screen us—
If you and I achieve a world of dream, complete in itself.

[1923]

52

Thunder Peak Pagoda
(Madame White of Hangzhou)

雷峰塔 (杭白)

"This is the ancient tomb of the White Snake."
(Boatman points to a thick and grassy grove);
"Folks, you know this old story of West Lake—
She was not human, but she fell in love.

"She loved a worthless bastard named Xu Xian.
She loved him and he listened to a priest—
Used an alms bowl to fix her in snake form;
She loved—and she got suffering without cease.

"Crushed beneath Thunder Peak a thousand years;
Left here; abandoned; underneath the ground
In this dreary decayed place—ruined—bare—
The evening bell tolls for her. Hear—It sounds."

[1923]

53

The two previous poems were inspired by ancient Thunder Peak Pagoda, site of events in the life of one of the great romantic heroines of Chinese legend and the subject of innumerable poems, operas, and movies. Madame White, a snake who had taken on the form of a woman, fell in love with and sacrificed everything for her husband, Xu Xian. For that transgression she lost the merit gained from hundreds of years of virtuous striving for *nirvana*, and was imprisoned under Thunder Peak Pagoda forever. The alms bowl referred to in the second poem is a holy object that changed her from a beautiful woman back into animal form; she was unable to prevent this because she had abandoned holiness for passion. According to some versions of the legend, she was defeated also because she was weak from being pregnant with Xu Xian's child. Xu Zhimo, who had deserted his own pregnant wife, leaving her alone in a foreign country (England), wrote three poems referring to this legend.

Thunder Peak Pagoda actually collapsed in 1924, after Xu wrote these poems, but was rebuilt in 2002. The poem's claim to be a "movie" was added to the title by Xu after its initial publication; the original title was *Thunder Peak Under the Moon.* This poem is indeed like a clip of a silent black-and-white film. When Xu uses "shadow" in the first line, he is punning—movies in Chinese are literally "electric shadows," or as here, "shadow pieces," so he is sending his lover both a movie in words and (figuratively) a piece of the shadow of the pagoda. In the second poem, Xu uses a coarse, countrified idiom imitating the speech of the boatman pointing out the landmark to a tourist. The third poem, *I Won't See Thunder Peak Again*, written after the collapse, is not included here.

Leifeng Ta (*Thunder Peak Pagoda*) in Hangzhou,
*originally built in 925, shown prior to its collapse in
1924. Image from Wikimedia Commons.*

Sayonara (Eighteen Poems)
沙扬娜拉十八首

1

I recall the dawn sun on the Fusang Sea
Scattered like gold.
I recall the islands floating like emeralds
On the Fusang—
Sayonara!

2

Board a boat in calm waves, see
Fishing boats of an old style
Skim bright waves like a flock
Of seabirds at sunset—
Sayonara!

3

A graveyard—whose? It blocks
The breeze; the view; the clouds; the pines' scent.
I do not forget that the tomb dwellers once
Also saw this pure scene; smelled these pines.
Sayonara!
(Cemetery in the mountains near Kobe)

4

Hear the greenfinch's voice break
In the wind. See the wide wings of an eagle pierce
The clouds. Lean on an old pine; squint
Ask the tomb dwellers about the pleasures of
  those still outside—
Sayonara!
(Cemetery in the mountains near Kobe)

I envy your health, your joy, your madness
As you all shout "*Arigato!*" together.
Flowers rain on the city. I'm glad I'm here.
Even the dancing butterflies: "*Arigato!*"
Sayonara!
 (Festival in Osaka)

Add the music of my dreams, now.
The sound of *geta*; sharp and clear and yet restrained—
Lovely, the street full of lamp light and shadows
"*Arigato!*" Voices leaping in the lamp shadows.
Sayonara!
(Festival in Osaka)

Just like the splendor seen at the Three Gorges
Hozugawa has the elegance of blue unbroken mountains,
And as it would at treacherous Foshan Gorge
The small boat shoots like an arrow through flying foam.
Sayonara!
(Hozu River Rapids)

Abandon turbulence; sail into ripples; calm
In the clear ripples, green mountain's lovely reflection.
Prop up the long oar, and stop in the heart of the wave--
In the waves, see the fish swim at their leisure.
Sayonara!

Tranquillity! And when the sound of the oars stops

Hear joy! In the green forest resounding

A thrush? A robin? Like a fragrant balm

That enters my bitter, thirsting heart.

Sayonara!

"*Uta*." Do not sneer at the travellers' madness,

Boatmen, but enjoy the scene, and

Drink a cup of *sake*, friends together,

"*Uta*." The mountain spirit does not mind the crudeness of the song.

Sayonara!

I won't dispute—so pointless—about different song styles.

Like lawless waves seen hissing in mountain caves,

Like an old soldier speaking of the days of his strength,

"*Uta, Uta*." My breast fills with wild thoughts.

Sayonara!

That's a cuckoo! She embroiders a silk sash

Which joins together the green bamboo trunks, the green mountain.

 In the emerald waves she leaves traces of her feet,

And the waves' beauty screens her shy peach blossom aura.

Sayonara!

But the happiness that made me drunk,

Was not only the deep azalea fragrance.

But the pretty and gentle girls,

Whose beauty surpasses the cuckoo's gentleness.

Sayonara!

I love their bodies' nimble gracefulness.
Natural beauties, they are natural beauties.
I love the colors matched so well in their clothing.
They are nimble like butterflies; butterfly beauties!
Sayonara!

Their beauty honors the Creator's skill;
The way they turn their eyes aside, so courteous.
Their freedom wafts like fragrance in warm winds,
Their smiles, their gentle airs—I can't get enough!
Sayonara!

I am a moth in a ravine
I take shape in the grass, fly in the dark
I offer up golden dust from my wings—
I am in love with a far away star.
Sayonara!

59

I am a drunken honeybee
Full of fragrance; insane, and I don't care
Now on the road back, humming in my small throat
I praise a brew from flowers I tried once—
Sayonara!

How fragile her head looks as she bows
Like a lotus too slight to face the chill winds.
She says: "Take care of yourself—please take care—"
Honeysweet sadness in the way she says "Take care."
Sayonara.

[1924]

Sayonara was written after Xu's trip to Japan with Tagore in May 1924, just after the Nobel laureate's visit to China. The eighteen-stanza poem was published in 1925 in *Zhimo's Poems*, his first volume of new verse. However, only the eighteenth stanza was republished in 1928, subtitled *To a Japanese Girl*. That stanza is very popular and still appears alone, although all eighteen stanzas were republished in Taiwan in 1980.

Sayonara can be seen as a companion poem to *On Leaving Japan* (following), written about the same time. In my opinion, it is a link between *Dewdrops on Grass* and many major poems to come, as Xu touches on many themes he will later develop. To note only the correspondences with *Cambridge, Farewell Again*, in this poem the poet bids farewell to a magical foreign place where he has had intense experiences; water is central to the action, as are boats (the word used for "oar" in stanzas 8 and 9 is the same used for the punting pole later in *Cambridge*); nature and the voices of insects and animals are key to the experience. But as in *Dewdrops*, the poet meditates on the nature of creativity, then metamorphoses so as to become creative. The poem is dense with allusions and double entendre, and contains Japanese words transliterated into Chinese. I kept these in Japanese, substituting the romanized spellings, and added *geta* for the distinctive wooden-soled sandals. *Sayonara,* of course means "farewell"; *arigato* is "thank you"; and *uta* means "song."

The poem is clearly not just about one woman, and the first stanza makes it clear that what he is writing about is already a memory, which he emphasizes through the repetition of *sayonara* after each stanza. Stanzas 1 and 2 recall Xu's arrival in Japan and his first boat excursion. He uses the old word for Japan, Fusang, as he did in *On Leaving Japan*. However, he still manages to refer to Japan's modern name in Chinese (and in Japanese) as 日本, literally meaning "sun origin," while never using those characters, by making the first stanza take place as the "dawn sun" is rising. The second stanza takes place as the sun sets, the first contrasting image in this poem full of contrasts. In these opening stanzas he also introduces much of the imagery—boats, birds, calm (versus turbulence) and emeralds (or jasper), gold, and green—which will be important throughout. As an example of his many untranslatable devices, the image of stars is introduced in the second stanza by using the "measure word" (a grammatical form in Chinese) *xing* for boats, which has the meaning of "star" as well.

Stanzas 3 and 4 take the reader to the land, as opposed to the water, specifically to a graveyard on the top of Mount Kobe. Here Xu asks questions about life and death, the same questions he asks in his *Elegy for Mansfield* and elsewhere. As he ponders on what the dead experience, as their graveyard blocks the breeze and the view, he keeps repeating the words *qingming*, literally "pure and bright." To a Chinese, these words in a cemetery invoke that festival on the first day of the fifth month in the lunar calendar, when ancestral graves are cleaned. Xu repeats these two words throughout the poem as well as another *qing* (青, pronounced the same as the 清 in *qingming*) which can mean blue, green, black, or dark, and can also mean fresh greenery or new plants, depending on context.

The cemetery on the mountain near Kobe houses the departed and is tranquil; the pines, a symbol of longevity, are mentioned three times before the poet pivots to the exuberance and noise that the living are making at a festival taking place in Osaka. Wooden clogs clop on the street beneath the worshippers' feet and Xu envies their health and vitality. He also envies their "madness." Creativity is madness of a sort, of course, and madness has interesting connotations in traditional Chinese culture. Those enlightened in Buddhism or who have found the the Way (Dao) often appear mad to ordinary folk.

The poet then goes to the Hozu River Rapids (compared to similar rapids in China on the Three Gorges), where the woods are again *qing* (green?) as is the mountain, and the water when not turbulent is also *qing* (clear or pure). At that point, the tension between opposites is even more evident as the turbulence of the rapids and the tranquility of the quiet spot on the water where one can stop the boat with one's "punting pole" are right next to each other, and the reflection of the mountain can be seen in the ripples of calm water, just as Mont Blanc could be seen in Lake Geneva in the poem written to eulogize Katharine Mansfield. It is implied that the reflection can perhaps help Xu to perceive something he cannot directly comprehend (in the Mansfield poem, death and life—here, the same perhaps, but definitely creativity). Xu does not attempt to embrace the reflection, in the manner of the greatest Chinese poet Li Bai, who drowned trying to embrace the reflection of the moon in water.

He does, however, like Li Bai, get drunk, although on the exotic foreign liquor, *sake*. He wants to share this with the boatman (or boatmen) whom he asks not to mock his madness. Able now to sing, like the worshippers at the festival, like the thrush or robin whose "loud joy" he just heard (even though it is a different kind of song and perhaps crude) Xu thinks that nature, in the form of the mountain spirit, will approve.

The cuckoo is not singing but is binding natural things together, bamboo to mountain. Xu makes use of the fact that the word for this sort of cuckoo (*dujuan*) and the word for azalea or rhododendron are the same in Chinese, as the azalea is the "cuckoo" flower. The *dujuan* is symbolic in China, but Xu's imagery is not traditional. He used the *dujuan* often in poetry. The very first poem we have, that he wrote as a school exercise, has this for a subject and in 1931 he wrote one of his last poems, addressed to the "passionate" cuckoo.

This particular cuckoo has left her footprints in the emerald (or jasper) water. "She" (modern Chinese, unlike classical, can be used to let the reader know a sex and Xu makes use of this—is described as beautifully shy and delicate and "shaded" by the waves (in another untranslatable image) like a peach blossom bud. The peach also symbolizes longevity, as well as spring. Here "she" leads him to bring up the subject of Japanese maidens, who are even more delicately beautiful. Xu longs to pursue them. He describes himself taking shape in the grass as a "night butterfly" that dusts flowers with the golden pollen on his wings, and then becoming a drunken honey bee "swollen" with fragrance in imagery that is not merely symbolically sexual, but is, as in *Dewdrops on Grass*, comparing the sexual urge with the creative urge. Unlike in that first poem, however, the creative urge here can reach its fruition. In spite of his desire for romantic relationships with the women of Japan, Xu tells the reader that he remains in love with a bright and very distant star and does not forget a single flower whose "brew" he formerly tried.

In the exquisite last stanza, for so long published as if it were a single poem, it is clear that the Xu persona has left one woman in Fusang who is sad that he is leaving. Poignantly, the girl who bids him farewell—*Sayonara!*—is compared to a lotus, a symbol of purity, as it remains unsoiled in spite of growing from the mud.

Hozu River in Early Summer, *from the series "New Selection of Noted Places of Kyoto" by Miki Suizan, 1924. Courtesy of the Lavenberg Collection of Japanese Prints.*

The Ancient Tribe of Hua

On Leaving Japan
留別日本

I am ashamed that I come from an ancient, cultured land
I am ashamed—my blood is that of such an ancient race
I am ashamed that filled with filth now Yang-tse waters flow
I am ashamed, when Mount Fuji, so pure, so clean, I face—

I imagine, quite often, times of old and the strength of Tang—
The moon's color over Luoyi; the bright sun on Chang'an,
At Wu Gorge the waves' voices; on Shu Road the jackals' cries;
And the *pipa's* weak complaining in the deep night near Xunyang—

But we can't imitate the beauty of the ancient tribe of Hua;
We can't see. A thousand years of confusion make us blind.
Where was it from, the crazy wind that destroyed the old life and art?
I feel fear when the white bones on Central Plain come to my mind!

I'm a yellow leaf floating in the wind—in the whirlwind I float
And recall the colossus of past times; all bare and withered now—
I'm an unlucky water drop; in deep, deep mud I crawl,
Yet in this dry old mountain stream, living water used to flow.

I want to be the spring wind—the spring wind that boasts of life,
    To shock out of delusive dream this giant, lonely tree—
    I want a shovel that won't bend, to dig up mud and slime—
And let gush forth, to drench the world, this huge hid stream, set free!

    So I envy this island, keeping her customs from ancient times,
    In her countryside I see strength; elegance; purity—
    I pray that my own land will rise again, but I also desire
The dawn's glow in the east to preserve for always the *fusang*'s beauty!

        [1924]

This poem was written in 1924, after Xu journeyed to Japan with Rabindranath Tagore. In fact, its complaint echoes one of Tagore's most well-known poems, *Where the Mind is Without Fear*, the last line of which pleads "Let my country awake." This is not one of Xu's ironical or humorous poems: He states and repeats three times that he is ashamed to be Chinese, and sets up a strong contrast between China and Japan, which seems at first to be in Japan's favor. By the second stanza, however, the reader realizes that it is not. Although honestly describing her flaws, Xu obliquely, and very beautifully, begins to extoll China's past glory.

    The Tang dynasty (618–907 A.D.) was arguably China's greatest period of cultural flowering, famed among other things for its poetic achievements. In the second stanza, Xu refers to Chang'an and Luoyi (present day Xian and

Luoyang) both capitals of the dynasty. He then refers obliquely to poems by the three great masters of poetry in the Tang period: Du Fu, Li Bai, and Bai Juyi. Du Fu mentions Wu Gorge in his poem *Autumn Meditation*; Li Bai wrote a poem called *The Roads to Shu are Hard*; and Bai Juyi wrote the *Ballad of the Pipa*, a stringed instrument similar to a lute or guitar. Wu Gorge is one of the famous Three Gorges, important in the poem *Sayonara*, p. 56.

Hua (華) is one of the oldest names Chinese have for their nation and themselves, while the Central Plain is the ancient cradle of Chinese civilization. The *fusang*, although sometimes translated as "hibiscus," is actually a mythical tree that has come to symbolize Japan, because it is said to flower on an island where the sun rises, to the east of China.

Except for the statements about his personal shame, nothing is said directly, but everything is made completely clear and the reader is the more strongly aware of Xu's intense patriotism (and despair) because of his country's lack of direction. Thus, in the fifth stanza, when Xu bursts out passionately with what he wants to do for China ("I want a shovel that won't bend, etc.") the impact is strong. And yet the final stanza is quiet, elegiac. In it, Xu expresses his hope that Japan may survive forever (this was written long before the Japanese aggression against China in the 1930s); however, he makes his preference for his own country very clear in his wish for the renewed glory of "my own land."

It's Rare

难得

It's rare that a night is so tranquil
It's rare that the stove is so warm
And rare that kindred spirits meet with no need for speech,
    A pair of usually lonely souls.

There is no need to plan or manage
No need for any critiquing at all
Facing the fire, no jealousy, hate or pride, and calmly
    Counting the cries of the night watch, afar.

Please drink a mouthful of clean water
My friend, and moisten your dry mouth.
Add some more coal to the red flames inside of the stove,
    Friend, it is grateful for your attention.

As on this icy winter night, friend,
We've just begun to know the worth of the stove,
The same way, in this ice-cold world, we know how few
    Is the number of sympathetic souls.

[1925]

Mister! Mister!

先生！先生！

Wheels made of steel
Fly fast through narrow, hidden street
"Mister—may I pay my respects—Mister—Mister—"

Squatting there in front
A lone girl in cloth pants with a quavering voice—
Wheels white like ice in the cold north wind fly.

Following close, close—
Ragged child chasing gleaming, gleaming wheels—
"Mister—have pity—you are kind—kind Mister!"

"Have pity on my Ma—
She's hungry, frozen, ill; she lies stretched out on the roadside—
You're so good—give a bite of steamed bread—please—kind Mister."

"Didn't bring money belt,"
Says the man in the fur hat, in his rickshaw, enthroned—
Flying, quick whirring wheels, quickly chasing—child's voice—

Dust on the road whirls like wind.
In the dust, flying whirring wheels, shining like silver, shining bright—
"Mister—you didn't come out without money—please sir—Mister—"

"Mister—Mister—"
The rushing child gasps—her voice fading, distant now—
Flying, flying rubber wheels don't stop flying—

Flying—Mister—
Mister—flying—
Mister—Mister—
Mister—

[1923]   *69*

| See Introduction p. 20 for comments on this poem.

Plum Blossom and Snow Compete for Spring
(In Memory of March 18th)

梅雪争春 (纪念三一八)

Early this year, in the south, snow fell heavily.
I went to Ling Feng, asking for news of the flowers.
Cruelly fallen calyxes, plum petals were preserved in snow;
Smiling, I said: How resplendent, their color!

Fate answered me: You came to see the flowers here.
But I've prepared a spring scene in Beijing for you—
The white is fluttering, flying, cold snow;
The plum petals—a thirteen year old's blood.

[1926]

In traditional China the Lunar New Year, which takes place in late January or February, marks the beginning of spring, a time for flower viewing. The title refers to an old saying describing this season, when plum flowers may bloom even while snow is falling. On March 18, 1926, a group of soldiers from the Beiyang army fired into an unarmed crowd, killing more than forty students, the youngest thirteen, and wounding more than two hundred.

Who Knows?

谁 知 道

Late at night a rickshaw to return home.
An old man in rags dragging my cart—
Not a star in the sky
And no light in the street
And the small gleam of light from the cart
Rushes at the earth in the street's heart as
The rickshaw man takes quick, small steps,
Stumbling left—stumbling right—

"Hey! Rickshaw man! Tell me—this street—why is it so dark?"
"Isn't it so, sir? This street's dark, isn't it—really dark."
He drags. Drags me down the street; then, through an arch.
Turns a corner, another corner; and it's all dark—
Not a star in the sky
And no light in the street
And the small gleam of light from the cart
Cheats the earth in the street's heart as
The rickshaw man takes quick, small steps,
Stumbling left—stumbling right—

Hey! Rickshaw man! It's so silent this street. Why no noise?"

"Isn't it so, sir? This street's silent, isn't it? There's no noise."

He drags. Long as the Great Wall is the wall he crowds against,

        dragging me along—

And we cross the river's edge. Turn. We're in a wilderness, black and far—

        Not a star in the sky

        And no light in the street

        And the small gleam of light from the cart

        Sways at the earth in the street's heart as

        The rickshaw man takes quick, small steps,

        Stumbling left—stumbling right—

"Hey! Rickshaw man! It's deserted, this street. No one's here. Why not?"

"That's not so, sir. Look again. You haven't looked carefully; not at all."

        I look—and inside my bones the marrow turns cold.

Green and circling like smoke, can they be human? Are they ghosts?

        I hear deep, throaty voices, chuckling growls—

The ground here is thick with graves! It was like this, all along—

        Not a star in the sky

        And no light in the street

        And the small gleam of light from the cart

        Circles on the earth in the street's heart as

        The rickshaw man takes quick, small steps,

        Stumbling left—stumbling right—

"Hey! Rickshaw man! Hey! Why is—why's this street so far?"
"Isn't it so, sir? The street is far away. Really far."
"But—I was going home. Have you lost the way?
"Who knows, sir? Who ever knows if they've lost the way. Or not?"
Late at night, a rickshaw to return home.
A crowd of men, in rags, dragging carts;
Not a star in the sky
And no light in the street
And the small gleam of light from the cart
Curls upwards from the earth in the street's heart as
The rickshaw men take quick, small steps,
Stumbling left—stumbling right—

[1924]   73

| *You Go* (p. 121) makes an interesting comparison to this poem.

Cricket

秋 虫

Cricket, why have you come? It's a long time
Now since, in this world, we have had leisure;
The green grass, the white dew are foolish, too;
Subjects for poems completely without use.
For yellow gold is all men cherish now,
It rules the day and it reigns over dreams,
And Love, like stars that linger in daylight
Flees quickly, so her shadow is not seen.
When the sky blackens, she does not return
But hides forever behind stormy clouds;
Integrity, too, in the desert conceals
Himself. Making that, for the present, his new home.
The flowers exhaust themselves in blossoming
And bear no fruit; while suffering Thought
By Theory is seduced and is raped.
Don't say these days in melancholy pass,

The face of bad luck follows from behind—
     As for the Soul, he's full of laziness:
He loves to hide in a garden and plant,
     He says "Don't listen as the rest all fall
Towards ugliness; changing to curs, worms, toads,
     Changing to swine. In a short time
The sun, ashamed, will give over his face; the moon
     Will not wish to be round anymore,
          When that day comes—
And Charity destroys what we now plant
I come again on that day, come to strike
     The bell that tolls out Revolution!"

                                        [1927]

| See Introduction p. 28 for comments on this poem.

Praise Offering

拜獻

Mountain—I do not laud your strength,
And Sea—I don't sing of your breadth.
Storm, I don't praise your power, which has no end—
But you, frail flower struggling in fields of snow
And you, the widow standing by the road
With the orphan; in blindness, voiceless—
And you, young swallow in the desert, burned
While returning home—To you— I sing in praise—
With the heat in my breast, blood in my veins, light in my soul.
May sunset clouds at the sky's edge weave a ribbon of joy for you,
May the rainbow, like a bridge, rise up and point eternally—
To a place where the light of this song's brightness extinguishes
Your endless, bitter loneliness . . .

[1929]

From *The West Window*

西窗

This west window,
This tactless west window lets in
Rays of afternoon sun at three o'clock
Which, slanted and straight, blend together on top of my bed;

Lets in a trouble-making bit of wind
Which embraces the virginal embroidered curtain,
Scratches her, embraces her waist, touches her neck,
Even her face; and when she tries to evade, blows her high in the air . . .

[1928]

77

These are the two first stanzas of a lengthy poem that uses the "west window" as metaphor, and in a series of of powerful images, talks about what it lets in. At the end Xu expresses his distress about those who, like fox spirits in Chinese myth, intend to drink the blood of the youth they stir up, once they have successfully used them to bring revolution to China.

LOVE

Susu

苏苏

Susu was senselessly in love.
Like a wild rose, she bloomed—
And as she bloomed, like a wild rose,
The wind and rain destroyed her.

There in that barren place is Susu's grave—
Drowned in the weeds. In the grass.
Her sorrow's drowned in the thick, wild grass—
And she's returned; a rose, blood-colored.

That rose's soul is senselessly in love—
In the morning, it receives the pure dew;
At dusk, caresses from the evening wind
In the long night, it sees the endless stars.

You say, she has the peace now she deserves—
Yes—but fate sends again a despoiler—
A hand plucks the radiance from the green stem—
Alas! Susu meets cruelty again!

[1925]

The character for the name Susu can mean "wild red basil," "revival," or, unusually, "reincarnation," although that last best fits the theme of this poem. See *Liebestod* (p. 122) for a similar use of the theme of killing roses by plucking them for their beauty, and *A Night in Florence* (p. 124) for the idea of lovers and reincarnation, widespread in Chinese literature. Lin Daiyu, the heroine of *Dream of the Red Chamber* (*Hong Lou Meng*) was the reincarnation of a celestial flower.

Midnight, Dark Alley, Pipa

半夜深巷琵琶

Again awakened by it from my dreams;

That *pipa* in the darkness of the night—

Whose grief is it?

Those fingers—whose?

Like cold wind; like sad rain; like flowers falling—

This time of night,

The time when dreams confound—

Do, re, mi, fa—plucking taut strings, playing confusion;

Harmonizing dark night, deserted street;

While from the willow branch there hangs the moon,

Oh—setting half wheel of a moon, like shattered hope; he wears

A torn hat on his head,

Is chained with steel,

Leaps like a lunatic on Time's path—smiles, insane—

"It's late," he says, "better blow out your light;

She waits on that other side of the grave

Waits for your kiss; your kiss; your kiss; your kiss."

[1926]

The *pipa* is a stringed instrument similar to a lute; in traditional poetry, *pipa* players are often beautiful women, who arouse feelings of romantic love in the poet. One of the most famous poems on the subject, by Bai Juyi of the Tang dynasty, is referred to in *On Leaving Japan* (p. 64). In the torn hat, rattling his chains, is the companion of the god of death as described in Chinese myth and folklore.

Song of Dead Leaves

落叶小唱

A rustling on the edge of the stairs
(As I approach the boundary of dreams)
Her footsteps now at last, I believe—
In the deep night!

A light knocking sound here on my window
(I press closer to the border of sleep)
She wants to disturb me—but as you see
I am still calm!

A sound of breathing comes near to my bed
I say (half in a dream, half in a daze)
"You never understand—and why do you
Keep hurting me!"

A sound of sighing now on my pillow
(I try to stay inside of dream's country)
"I wounded you," you say; and your hot tears
Burn on my cheek.

Noises disturb my spirit, locked in dream—
(In the courtyard the dead leaves dance and dance)
The dream is over; I awake; my pain
Just autumn's sounds.

[1925]

I've Come to the Yang-tse River . . .

我来扬子江边买一把莲蓬

I've come to the Yang-tse River to buy lotus.
My hands peel it—one layer, then the next;
I see the river gulls as they pass, flying;
Endure the feeling of tears filling my eyes
Thinking of you, thinking of you, ah—Xiaolong!

Tasting the lotus flesh. Remembering the flavor from before—warm—
Remembering the screen, in front of the stairs, never rolled up
That hid our joy, our pleasures when we were one;
And I hear once again your promises—
"I'm yours. Yours. Body. Soul. Forever. Yours."

Tasting the lotus heart. My heart's more bitter.
I lie awake, these long nights, sleepless and scared—
The nightmares don't stop. I can't break free.
This agony I have inside—who understands it?
I can't get through my days, love—such pain—

But I can't blame you. I can't bear to suspect you've changed.
I only have feelings of softness.
You *are* mine. Just like before
I want to tightly, tightly keep and hold you
Unless the sky turns upside down; and that, who can imagine?

[1925]

The poet is buying not the flower but the cupule of the lotus plant, which has seeds that he peels and eats. However, these seeds are bitter. In Chinese, to "eat bitter" or "to have a bitter heart" means to feel great grief, or undergo great hardship. *Xiaolong* means "little dragon," a reference to Xu's future wife, Lu Xiaoman. In an August ninth diary entry of the same year, the poet writes of her, "you are truly nimble, truly vivacious, you are truly like a little dragon." Xiaoman is also associated in other poems with the lotus flower, which represents purity (see *The Carp Leaps*, p. 95, and *She Sleeps*, p. 92).

Little Poem

小 诗

Moon: bashfully I say
Take note, please, of the hot and cold tears I've shed
In your special record of love and sorrow.

Moon: sobbing I request
That you inspect the chart showing my tears discharged
Is it a new account, or have I paid my debt?

[1922]

As discussed in the Introduction (p. 25), Xu's use of ironic distance saves him from ever coming across as obnoxious and self-pitying. In this first poem of the many mentioning his tears, Xu addresses the moon, asking the heavenly body about its bookkeeping with regard to unhappy lovers. This is one of many images Xu draws from traditional Chinese literature and popular culture, where it is often seen, perhaps most famously in the novel *Dream of the Red Chamber (Hong Lou Meng)*, where the heroine must repay "a debt of tears" on earth before she can return to heaven, a debt connected with love. In the novel, the debt and the tears are taken with the utmost seriousness—but Xu's reader can tell at once that, while unhappy, he is still playful. "Is this a new account, or have I paid my debt?" he asks, after describing his "hot and cold tears" and the implication is "enough, enough." So Xu cries—but teases himself at the same time, and lets the reader know that he deserves ridicule if he cries too much.

Verse

诗句

Bright moon—your brightness not less than it was—
As—in this grove of olives—the nightingale's joy spills out—
Bright moon—bright on my tear-soaked pillow; kind; clean like dew—
My sadness is also not less than it was.

—Summer, 1925, in the hills near Florence

Coral

珊 瑚

You don't need to think I speak
My heart drowned in the sea's depths long ago
You don't need to shout at me
Because I—I can't respond.

Unless you—unless you also come to
This other world of coral bone revolving
Waiting for the sea wind's fixed moment of silence
When you and I can alternately sigh our hidden sighs.

[1925]

The White-Whiskered Old Man of the Sea
白须的海老儿

The ship casts anchor in the center of the sea.
It pays no heed to the fire that burns in me—
The old man of the sea, with his white beard, has pity, though;
In his soft voice asks, "Why not farther go?"

I stretch out my hands; I reach to hold emptiness.
In this haze, who can tell that I do not caress
Her waist? I blow toward the river in the sky
A kiss; the star she loves glows there like a bright eye.

But the white-bearded old man is now dismayed—
(He is jealous of the young, because of his age)—
He says: "Have I troubled you to no avail?
Jump— can you cross the limitless green waves?"

Mischievous old man, playing his odd tricks on me;
The heat in my heart almost became froth on the sea.
This time, I rush to kiss her fragrance once again.
But who can struggle with him twice—and win?

[1926]

Notification

消息

Thunder has stopped for a time;
And in clouds; in fog—
Rainbows—two dragons—
Lively; vivid; bright—
Good news! Tomorrow's
Weather fine—

What! Again thunder [clap]—
Outside clouds and sky—
Darkness now again—
Rainbows' hues not seen—
And feeble-footed Hope
Vanishes.

[1924]

87

I Don't Know Which Way the Wind Blows
我不知道风是在哪一个方向吹

I don't know
Which way the wind blows;
I am in a dream—
In dream's waves whirling about.

I don't know
Which way the wind blows;
I am in a dream—
Her tenderness; my intoxication.

I don't know
Which way the wind blows;
I am in a dream—
Sweet is the glory of my dream.

I don't know
Which way the wind blows;
I am in a dream—
Her ingratitude; my sorrow.

I don't know
Which way the wind blows;
I am in a dream—
In dream's sorrow, my broken heart.

I don't know
Which way the wind blows;
I am in a dream—
Darkened the glory of my dream.

[1928]

Untitled

无 题

Oxherd, and Weaving Maid—
Kept separate by water pale and clear.
No words, when these two meet—
Just resurgence of overflowing love.

[1925]

The Oxherd and the Weaving Maiden are the stars Vega and Altair. In Chinese legend, they are separated by the Milky Way, which the Chinese call the Silver River. They are allowed to meet only one night in the year as punishment for having been so much in love that they neglected their heavenly duties. The Qixi Festival (also called Double Seven) that celebrates their annual meeting is akin to Valentine's Day in China. See "Oxherd and Weaving Maiden" in my *Repairing the Sky.* This charming little poem was jotted down by Xu in his famous *Loving Eyebrows Diary* (written during his courtship of Lu Xiaoman), which was not published until 1945. It is dated August 31, which may have been the date of Qixi in 1925. "Eyebrows" (*Mei*) was Xiaoman's nickname and an ancient way of referring to a beautiful woman.

In the Mountains

山中

The courtyard's peaceful,
Though one hears the noise of the city, all around.
The moon shines brightly,
The shadows of the pines are like embroidery on the ground.

I do not know what
Can be seen in the mountains where you are.
I assume there is also the moon, and also pines
And that peace overflows.

I want to grasp moonlight,
Transform it into clean wind; pure—
I want to blow awake a flock of pine trees, drunk with spring,
And waft them to the mountains, where you are.

And there, green like an emerald,
On your window a single pine needle will fall.
Gently; as gentle as a sigh,
And it won't startle you out of your sleep at all.

[1931]

She Sleeps

她是睡着了

She sleeps
Like a white lotus lying in starlight
She has entered the place of dreams
Blue smoke from the censer wafts softly up.

She slumbers soundly
Sound of a mountain stream blocks the *qin's* sounds
She's in dream's kingdom
Pink and green butterflies hover around.

Her breathing pauses
A soothing scent enters the air
Surrounding her; it's pure, it's blessed
And palpable, embraces her slim form.

Luxurious moment! In its tranquillity
Precious like shining gold.
It stretches from here to eternity
In spite of waves that furiously toss our boat.

I am intoxicated when I see her
I want to sip wine, put on my best clothes
Pluck flowers from the wisteria bough
And dance, as if I trod grapes, till I fall.

How very lovely!
On her smooth skin, the colors of spring bloom
Roses, beautiful roses
And fresh beauty of narcissus in the sun.

The dark secret beneath dream
Teases at her heart and at her pure soul,
Like a bee entering a flower—willful,
Impetuous, a little rude—yet soft.

How childlike is the place of dream!
Silence!—do not attract the attention of the dream god—
Pull one thread from the golden shuttle out—
From the silver net, a thread of silk for an evening cloud.

Jade wrist, gold shuttle
Weaving the finest of silks; but not for clothes
Silk that is transformed into sunset's colorful clouds—
Celestial palace—dance of angels—angel song.

Lovable dimples
Reveal a virgin's joy and virgin dreams
Just as the morning is reflected in the quivering
Of a pure dewdrop upon a lotus.

[1925]

The *qin* of the second stanza is a the traditional plucked zither that Xu mentions in many of his poems. The lotus denotes purity; the butterflies are symbols of marital bliss. The sound of the sleeper's precious slumber that follows is described by Xu as *"sha, sha"* in a beautiful (and untranslatable) onomatopoeia. The colorful clouds in the penultimate stanza refer to the Chinese legend that the sunrise and sunset clouds are woven by maidens in the Heavenly Palace under the supervision of the Western Queen Mother (see "Oxherd and Weaving Maiden" in my *Repairing the Sky*). However, immediately afterwards Xu uses the transliterated English word for "angels," clearly wanting to add Western (Biblical) imagery.

Snowflake Joy

雪花的快乐

Oh, if I were a snowflake,
Flying gracefully in the air,
I'd know where I was going
And I'd glide, glide, glide, glide—
To my goal down here.

Not a cold, lonely valley,
Not a mountain peak, chilly and pure
Not a street—sad—deserted—
I would glide, glide, glide, glide!
I know where.

I would dance in the ether
Till I saw the pure place where she dwells,
When she came to her garden,
I would glide, glide, glide, glide;
Ah, her skin, with its sweet, plum-like smell!

As a light, weightless snowflake,
I'd softly on her clothes come to rest.
I would lie on her beating heart—
And I'd melt, melt, melt, melt
On her breast.

[1924]

Considered to be one of Xu's most lyrical, this poem has clear echoes of Keats'
sonnet *"Bright Star, would I were stedfast as thou art."*

The Carp Leaps
鲤跳

You walked straight into a creek that day.
"I'll carry you," I said. You answered, "No."
"Let me help you across." Again, "No—
Go first; the water's lovely, I will stay.

"I want to be a fish! Or else grow
In Nature, like a blade of grass, sleep there—
And have no troubles, never shed a tear—
Look at me leaping like a carp! So!"

You left the water then, a shining flash.
Lightly your foot touched the ground, and you laughed
With your whole body; your willow waist swayed
And the water was filled with bright carp scales.

[1930]

The Chinese carp, known more widely by its Japanese name, *koi*, is an ancient symbol of abundance. A legend holds that when carp swimming up the Yellow River reach a place called Dragon's Gate, they can leap upwards and be transformed into dragons. This of course fits with Xu's recurring themes of transformation and human metamorphosis to become a part of nature. It is worth noting again that he described his second wife, Lu Xiao Man, as being like a dragon.

The Birth of Spring

春的投生

Yesterday evening
And also the evening before
In the savagery of a storm
Spring
Was born inside withered winter's corpse.

Don't you feel softness underfoot?
And warm softness around your hair and ears?
Greenness floats above on the tree branches
Beneath the pond, ripples of endless longing
And in your body and mine, in our limbs and breasts
An unaccustomed rhythm beats.

Already on your face, peach blossom blooms.
I am in ecstasy seeing your beauty, and I drink
The sound of your laugh.
Don't you feel my arms
Seeking your waist—urgent—and my breath
Aimed towards you, the way a million fireflies
Swarm at the light?

All of these things, and many others
Along with the passionate songbirds
All, all are united now praising
The birth of Spring.

[1929]

Critics have observed that fireflies do not swarm at lights. But Xu was not a scientist. Fireflies are an important symbol in many of his poems—in *A Night In Florence* (p. 124), the protagonist even wishes to be reincarnated as one.

Untitled

无题

To Lu Xiaoman

You're part of my heart now, flesh of my flesh
My life has reached its longed for destination!
I see the white clouds fly on the horizon,
I hear the sparrows crying on the branch
And can't stop giving thanks. And with hot tears—
I gratefully sigh.
I know contentment, now.
And don't desire any more from heaven.

[1926]

98

This was included in a letter dated February 23, 1926, to Lu Xiaoman, but not published until 1987.

Don't Pinch, It Hurts . . .

别 拧 我, 疼 ...

"Don't pinch, it hurts . . ."
You say, and the space between your brows slightly closes.

That "hurts"—a round essence half spat out
Turning, sliding on tongue.

Eyes also seem to speak;
In their brightness ripples rise
Secrets from the fountain of your heart.

Dreams
Wine bottle opened
Light gauze mosquito net . . .

"Are you there—?"
"Make us die," you say.

[1931]

See Introduction p. 18 for comments on this poem.

A Hero Like a God
天神似的英雄

Those stones, piled up, all ugly, not one stands out—
That lily, though—loveliest in the grove—
When moonlight traces flower's shadow on stone,
How lovely then, how resplendent the stone!

I'm just an average guy, just one in a crowd;
Her beauty, though—miraculous—matchless—
And when she nestles, in love, soft on my breast—
I become a hero—become a god!

[1927]

The Last Day
最后那一天

In the year that the spring wind does not blow,
The day the winter branches don't turn green,
At the time that the sky does not grow bright
    In the black mist, and chaos overwhelms
The sun, moon, stars extinguished in the void;
That day, when all that's normal is cast down,
    That time, with values re-evaluated
        And vanity, deceit and emptiness
Are all exposed in final, stern judgment;
When souls, naked and prostrate, face the Lord—
    On that day you and I, love, need not fear
Nor explain, nor appeal and much less hide.
Your heart and mine, twin flowers on one green stalk
Called Love, will stand upright, in beauty, fresh delight.
    In front of the Lord, Love is the only Glory.

[1927]

This is a Coward's World
这是一个懦怯的世界

It does not allow love, allow love.
Darling, take down your hair,
And let your feet go bare
And follow me! We'll die
Throwing the world away; love's sacrifice.

Follow; I'll hold your hand
As tightly as I can
Though thorns rip at our feet
And hail and frozen sleet
Strike our heads, follow me
Hold hands and we'll break free
Out of man's world, this prison!

Follow me!
Love!
The world at our backs—See
The wide, wide white sea
The huge and wide white sea
You, I and love—endlessly free.

Come—lift your head and look
At that star on the blue horizon.
The island there, green grass—
Lovely flowers, beasts, birds—
Let's take our little boat
And sail to heaven; Let's go
To everlasting love and joy and freedom.

[1925]

Bang!

丁当一请新

What does the autumn rain say, on the eaves?
"Drop her now, let her go; why should you grieve?"
Then bang! I drop a mirror on the ground
And it breaks, with a violent sound.

Now what does it say, the autumnal rain?
It asks: "What will you do with those remains
Inside your heart?" Then, again that loud sound—
"Bang!" and my heart lies broken on the ground.

[1925]

Late at Night

深夜

Late at night, a street corner.
Street light shines brightly just like in a dream.

Even the trees get lost in this fog, thick as smoke.
Is it surprising people can't find their way?

"You hurt me—I hate you!"
She sobs; he—doesn't answer.

Dawn wind gently shakes the tops of the trees.
Fallen; the early autumn's crimson splendor.

[1928]

104

Lin Daiyu Burying Flowers, *painting on silk by Fei Danxu (1801–50),
depicting the heroine of* Dream of the Red Chamber *in a scene well known
to Chinese readers.*

Waning Spring

残春

I put peach blooms in a vase, yesterday,
Lovely like a smile on a beauty's face.
Today their heads are bent, and they have changed.
Pink and white corpses droop on the green vase.
Outside the window, sounds of wind and rain
Chime like bells that warn the spring of its fate.
In your life's vase, the flowers have also changed.
Who'll dress those lovely corpses for the grave?

[1927]

This rhyming poem was written in Xu's diary dated April 20, 1927, but then published in both *Crescent* magazine and in the volume *Tyger.* A year earlier Hu Shi, a close friend, had written a poem titled *Flowers in a Vase* for Xu's second wife, Lu Xiaoman. That poem borrowed imagery from a well-known poem by Song-dynastry poet Fan Chengda (1126–93) and Xu's poem uses the same images of wind, rain, and plucked flowers in a vase with petals falling. Xu introduces the theme of late spring by identifying the flowers as peach blossoms, now "corpses," and speaks of their "grave." Any flower "funeral" would recall to every Chinese the iconic scene of Lin Daiyu burying fallen petals in *Dream of the Red Chamber*; she then composes a poem, with Jia Baoyu composing one in reply. For those interested in comparing all three poems, Michelle Yeh translates the other two in her *Anthology of Modern Chinese poetry*, p. 12.

Whispers

私语

Autumn rain in a chilly autumn pond;
On a haggard branch of autumn willow,
On an anxious autumn bough,
On an autumn leaf, speckling yellow.
Listen to it. Breathy and intimate—
As it whispers three autumns' worth of passion and passionate thoughts—
Then let it fall into the autumn waves; spin around, drain away—
with Autumn—
The whispers of this autumn rain; three autumns' worth of passion and
passionate thoughts—
Passionate poems and stories of passion—
Let them too fall into the autumn waves, spin around and drain away—
with Autumn.

[MS DATED] JULY 21, 1922

A Quatrain

四行诗一首

Like a musician daily practicing
He plucks at my heart, sincere in his grief;
Sorrow—calling out loud, and surging—wild—
Like a huge wild wave flying at a reef.

[1925]

Listening to the Piano Late at Night

月夜听琴

Whose song is this?
Whose melancholy notes
Do I hear in the shadow of the pines
As I walk lonely under shining stars?

Vibrations; an earthquake of song
Pierces the deep sorrow of the dark night
Tartarus black; and the dewdrops on grass
Cause torment deep inside of my sad soul.

I hear—I hear—I hear and comprehend
The instrument's grief; musician's sad heart
And in the tree branches up high above
My turmoil causes the shocked birds to wonder.

Stop complaining about her ice-cold heart
She does weep for you.
Stop saying that she is indifferent,
Her frozen breast is filled with flames of love.

Remember? Her face when you had to part?
Her eyes filled with softness, her acid tears,
You gripped her hand and felt its vibrations—
Nerves pulsing with love—

Remember? Your mood when you had to part?
The icy glacier that engulfed you whole.
The despair in your breast, the sea of tears—
Your soul, a prisoner shut up in sadness.

Oh, wind soughing so loudly in the pines
Stop disturbing my passionate listening!—
In the sea of this life, with how many tears
Will love drown my heart?

And up above, the brilliant autumn moon
Has stripped itself now of the clouds, its clothes
It seems to smile as it declares aloud:
"Love is man's life force!"

Oh, my passionate companion! I envy
The honey-sweet fire of your love.
But how fortuitous! the piano, the dusk
Link our souls, now; this moment.

[1923]

Lin Huiyin and Xu Zhimo.

Hearing the Sound of Music Late at Night

深夜里听到乐声

Surely those are your fingers, once more
Playing softly,
Late at night; in deep, secret sadness.

I can't help blushing as I
Softly listen
Late at night to the vigor of those strings.

And one note pierces my listening heart
With sorrow—
I understand; but how can I respond?

Long ago Life drafted this design.
Too fragile
Is the vision of beauty in this world.

Unless in dream perhaps one day
You and I might
Touch hope together, playing on that string.

[1931, WRITTEN BY LIN HUIYIN]

The eighteenth-century novel *Dream of the Red Chamber (Hong Lou Meng)* so often cited here uses the story of the decline and fall of an aristocratic family as an analogy to sum up five-thousand years of Chinese culture. The story's hero, Jia Baoyu, constantly praises the superior talent hidden in the women's quarters; the *hong lou* of the title refers to those "red chambers," where the female members of the family lived secluded. The author, Cao Xueqin, takes us inside to introduce his heroines, the "twelve beauties of Jinling," revealing their daily lives, in which composing poetry is a favored occupation. Their marvelous poems take up a large part of the narrative, more than would be tolerated in a comparable Western work. What Cao describes in this fictional context has been verified by the work of scholars such as Kang-i Sun Chang and Dorothy Ko: it was not at all unusual for elite women in traditional China to write. Moreover, their writing, including poetry, was often of a high standard and contributed to a family's glory—so long as it was never published, for strangers to see.

When Xu Zhimo sought to redirect Chinese poetry to assume a modern role, and to cast poets as poet-philosophers, he did not envision that women would be excluded as a result. The man whose master's thesis at Columbia University was on "The Status of Women in China" wanted to encourage women to write, and in this he was not violating the norms of traditional Chinese culture. He did transgress, however, when he allowed women such as Ling Shuhua (a May Fourth fiction writer who later became a member of the Bloomsbury group in England) to join the Crescent Club; to meet with men who were not her relatives; to read their works in public; and to take part in literary discussions. He further transgressed when he encouraged women to publish (as he did with the shy Pearl S. Buck) and when he published them himself in the influential literary magazines that he founded and edited. Of course, other male writers in this iconoclastic time were transgressing in these ways, too, but Xu went above and beyond.

Lin Huiyin was the woman he mentored who achieved the greatest success as a poet. Lin was a special case, because Xu had fallen in love with her and after divorcing his wife hoped to marry her. As Tony S. Hsu has pointed out in *Chasing the Modern*, Xu undoubtedly wished that he and Lin could be a couple like Elizabeth Barrett and Robert Browning. Xu idolized and idealized this literary pair, and especially admired Mrs. Browning, whose poetry he translated. I believe that this was not only because of her literary achievements, but also because her life story appeared a corrective to the wrecked romance at the heart of *Hong Lou Meng*. Lin Daiyu, the novel's heroine and the most talented poet among the twelve beauties, is clearly meant to be Jia Baoyu's mate. His elders, however, cannot see past her flaws and force him to marry the perfect woman—whom he does not love. Xu's solution was, of course, his Western-style divorce, but this did not make the beautiful, talented and sickly woman he loved elope with him. (Like both Lin Daiyu and Elizabeth Barrett, Lin Huiyin had poor health.) Rather than follow the model of Elizabeth Barrett, the object of his affections ran away from him. Only in later years, as a married woman, did Lin and her husband resume their friendship with Xu. Then Xu continued to nurture her literary talents. Lin would later tell Wilma Fairbank that she thought of Xu primarily as her "teacher."

Lin went on to become an important twentieth-century Chinese poet in her own right and I include this translation of one of her poems not only because of her master-pupil relationship to Xu, but because although they were written a few years apart, this particular poem I believe was written in answer to one of his. A poetic dialogue is not uncommon between traditional Chinese poets and of course is not unknown in the West. Presenting these poems in translation does, however, pose some problems. Since I translated both poems, they are likely to sound similar in style and in technique, which they are not. A false equivalence is more likely because, as is often the case with Xu, much of what he did in this work does not come across in English. Its tight form and brief length control a series of complex and powerful intertwined images and ultimately lead to philosophical questions that go far beyond what at first seems to be the subject. While Lin's poem is not simplistic, it is a great deal simpler. She only takes up one of the themes present in Xu. What she does with this theme is fascinating, though. Xu's poem puts his emotions on display. Lin recasts his words—reining those emotions in, bringing them under control. When she is done, she has managed to mute him. The volcanic dynamism of his self-expression is gone, though what she leaves is spare and much more orderly—and beautiful in its own way.

Let's look a little closer. Both pieces are instigated by listening to music at night. Xu hears piano music being played by a stranger as he walks by, undoubtedly some powerful romantic piece, perhaps Wagner (whose music inspired one of his poems). Hearing this music evokes intense emotions and immediately unites him, not just with the unseen, unknown musician, but with nature itself, feelings turbulent enough to compel "the shocked birds to wonder." He becomes lost in "earthquakes of sound" and feels intense "vibrations" coming from within. Later these vibrations are linked with the pulse of life-blood that he remembers feeling when he touched his lost lover, in spite of her "ice-cold heart."

Lin does not say what she is doing when *she* hears music. Although it is dark, the night, for her, is not the overpowering presence filled with stars, pine trees, dewdrops, and other personified entities that it is in Xu's poem. The music Lin hears is also sad, but she stresses that it is soft. She uses two different words for the softness, both used in Xu's *Second Farewell to Cambridge* (in my version translated as "softly" and "in silence"). It is worth noting that when Xu described softness and silence, in that iconic, contrasting poem it still contained swaggering plants, clouds that could possibly be carried off in a sleeve and insects that were, unusually, "struck dumb." Lin's poetic world is a great deal emptier than her teacher's, in short.

She, however, does tell us that she knows who the musician is in her poem, in contrast to Xu, where the player is unknown. "Surely those are *your* fingers." Lin does not allow the fingers to have "vigor," though. Only the instrument's strings. And she is very careful about admitting that anything at all has touched her. "One note" has "pierced" her heart, she says, but that is very different from admitting that her breast is "frozen" and "filled with flames of love." She certainly is not engulfed in icy glaciers, nor is she drowning in a sea of tears but the fact that she doesn't leave herself open to such strong emotions means that she is unable to follow Xu as he makes the astonishing progression from the shadow of the pines, the stars, and the dewdrops on the grass through the shocked birds and the hoarse wind soughing, to finally arrive at the point where the "brilliant" moon strips itself naked in front of him before it gives him the epiphany that "Love is man's life force." It smiles as it says this. And he achieves peace in the last stanza. He's no longer in Tartarus in this "fortuitous" moment; he feels his soul linked to the piano, the player and the dusk, though the lost lover is still lost. This is quite different (and a lot deeper) than Lin's hope of being united in dream "perhaps." The volcanic intimacy that Xu seeks, that comes from the complete comprehension possible only with true communication—Lin evades this delicately but entirely.

Lin Daiyu in *Hong Lou Meng* understood all about this kind of total communication, this intimacy beyond the physical— and on Baoyu's wedding day, she died. The fictional girl's poetry expressed *qing*, to use a Chinese term that Xu well understood, a term that might be loosely translated as "passion." Lin Daiyu is even said to be *duoqing*, a person with an excess of *qing*, something traditionally felt in China to be dangerous—but Elizabeth Barrett Browning expressed *duoqing* in her *Sonnets from the Portuguese*, and this did not kill her, it led to renewed life. Lin Huiyin did not accept either of these women as role models, though. Neither immured in the red chambers, nor shut up in a sick room in a house on Wimpole Street, but highly educated and well-traveled, Lin had her own goals and dreams and had to find her own ways to make them come true. When she entered the University of Pennsylvania in 1924, for example, she learned that women could not study architecture there, in the enlightened West. Her fiancé, Liang Sicheng, got the architecture degree, though that had been her dream before it was his, while Lin was forced to major in Fine Arts. She audited all the necessary classes and became the first female architect in China, anyway. "Life drafted this design," she says in the penultimate stanza of this poem, using a metaphor that relates to the career that she and her husband shared.

This poem was published in September 1931. In November, Xu crashed into Mount Tai, plummeted to earth in flames and died. He was on his way to see Lin—something that his former wife, Zhang Youyi, felt was not at all surprising. Lin asked her husband, who joined the search party, to bring her back a piece of the burned fuselage from Xu's plane. She hung it on their bedroom wall and kept it there for the rest of her life.

Complaint

怨得

Can't complain we met here—
Who caused it?—The wind!

A few words more now—
Dew wets the dry sprouts—

Darkness—Lightshaft like an arrow
Wounds a moth in flight—

Unexpected.
Why is it like this?—regret—

[1927]

Useless

枉 然

Useless, to seize on my mouth with your mouth;
It's useless to lock my hand in yours, too—
And your hot tears cannot convince me, now,
Nor your red blood, that what you say is true—

Too late! the dead can't be brought back to life;
And out of ashes raise up what's gone? How?
Woman, though God forgives you for your crime,
Even He has no love to give you now.

[1928]

116

Because

为的是

Woman,
   pray to you
    worship
    grovel
     Because . . . ?

Woman,
  ruined
   made foolish
    writing poems—for you—
     Because . . . ?

Woman,
  abuse,
   curses, lateness
   stepped on—
   Because . . .

       [1930]

What Kind of Thing is Love?
恋爱到底是什么一回事

After all, what kind of thing is love?
I had not yet been born when it came;
The sun shone on me more than twenty years,
I had no worries yet—I was a child;
Then, suddenly!—I love and loathe that day—
An itch inside my heart; discomfort,
And for the first time, then, I was deceived;
Wounded, some said—Feel there, touch my breast—
I had not yet been born when it came,
After all, what kind of thing is love?

I changed, became like an unbroken horse
Who could not be reined in, and I galloped
Across the wilderness of human life.
I was like the man from Chu in the tale, who
Offered his jade, finger pointing meanwhile
At his breast, saying, The truth is here. Truth!
If you don't believe me, cut my heart
Bleeding from my breast, see if it's not jade.
Blood! Cruel cutting open; oh, my soul!
Who compels me now to express this doubt?
Doubt! I'm glad to awake now from this dream.
Lord on High, I'm not ill and no longer
Do I groan before you. I do not wish
For apotheosis, nor Penglai.
I only want this earth; to be human.
I will not ask again, What is love?
Since I had not been born yet when it came.

[1928]

Kai–yu Hsu (*Twentieth Century Chinese Poetry*) thinks that this poem was writ-ten in 1925. It is difficult to translate because of its very specific Chinese imag-ery. Two conflated stories are referred to in the second stanza. First is the story of *Mr. He's Jade* (*Heshibi*), in which a man offered the most precious jade in the world to several kings, but was not believed and was punished by mutilation (see "The Treasure Worth Ten Cities" in my *Repairing the Sky*). The second story is of Daiyu's famous dream in chapter 82 of the classical novel *Dream of the Red Chamber*, in which the hero, Jia Baoyu, cuts his heart out and offers it to show her the sincerity of his love in the face of her continual doubts, which she seems compelled to keep expressing.

The language of Chinese Daoism and folk beliefs is seen here in the mention of "apotheosis" (literally, *cheng xian*, "to become an immortal)"; Penglai, (the Chinese Isle of the Blessed); and "the Lord on High" are also seen in *Onward, Forward* (p. 146).

At the beginning of the second stanza, Xu refers to himself as an "unbroken horse." He also refers to his pen this way in the preface to his *Tyger* (partially translated on p. 178), and refers to himself again in this way in the essay *My Grandmother's Death* (partially translated on p. 189). As a result, Chinese often affectionately refer to Xu Zhimo as an untamed, wild horse.

You Go

你去

You go; I'm leaving too, and here we part.
Take that highway—be at peace as you go—
The street lamps stretch straight to the horizon—
You just have to follow the line of light.
You go first. I'll stand here watching you go.
Take your time, and do not stir up the dust
I want to look at your shadow until
You've gone so far that I cannot see clear
And then—And then I shall scream out your name
Unceasingly; let you know I'm still here
And so dispel the deepening desolation
As I watch you go home . . .

                              But no! I don't
Want you to worry; You take that highway
I'll enter this alley. You look upwards
At that tree stretching to touch heaven while I
Turn and walk through chaos; desolation—
Further on there are deep pools, and ditches.
Ditches shiny with stagnant, dead water
Which in this boundless night seem like shed tears.
There are stone slopes, where weeds prick at one's legs
And those crossing the road can stumble; fall.
But do not be concerned, for if I'm brave
The dangers of the road won't chill my heart.
While you are distant, I will take great strides

The night dew in this desolation is pure.
Don't fret about the clouds, for the wind blows
Cinnabar from the stars to the cloud sea,
And furthermore, in the depths of my heart
You shine forever like a glowing pearl.
I love you!

[1931]

In the layered and complex ending to his poem, Xu literally says, "forever glows a *nightless* pearl," referring to the moon, in Chinese poetry sometimes called "bright pearl of the night." Xu is here suggesting that Lin Hui Yin, for whom the poem was written, is not the inconstant moon of the night sky, rather that of his own well-known poem, *Two Moons* (translated by Kai-yu Hsu in *Twentieth Century Chinese Poetry*, pp. 94–5), in which she is likened to a second moon that does not wane. Pearls were also thought to be able to preserve dead bodies, so this ending continues the medicinal themes brought up by the cinnabar (mercury), which was extensively used in traditional Chinese medicine, especially in elixirs of immortality.

Liebestod

情死

Roses; ovewhelming multitude of scarlet roses—last night's thunder and rain were your signal to come forth, you pampered beauties!

Your color is rich wine in my sight. I long to approach you, but don't dare.

Youth! There are white drops of dew on your foreheads—beauty spat out in the brilliance of dawn.

The smiles on your cheeks are brought from heaven; it's a shame that this vulgar world won't offer you the chance to stay here for long.

Your beauty is your doom.

I come closer. Your confusing, drunken fragrance and color enslave the soul—I'm your captive.

Over there, you smile your faint smiles. And over here, I tremble.

You look down below your feet into a deep and bottomless pond.

You stand by the side of the pond. I stand behind you—I, your captive.

And I faintly smile, over here. Over there, you tremble.

Beauty. Your doom. Your doom.

I've already taken you. Captured you in my hands. I love you, roses!

I take you—hold you in my hands—I love you, roses! But color fragrance
flesh soul beauty charm die as I clutch at them.

I tremble, here. While you—smile.

Roses; I can't bear to look as your jade beauty shatters and your fragrance is
snuffed out. I love you.

Petals, pistils, calyxes, thorns—you—I—what happiness!

123

Ending it glued together a welter of scarlet hands blurred with blood. Roses.
I love you.

[1923]

| See Introduction p. 29 for comments on this poem.

A NIGHT IN FLORENCE

A Night in Florence

翡冷翠的一夜

Tomorrow you are going to go? Then I—
Don't feel distressed. This day was bound to come.
Just—remember me. Please remember me.
Or else, please soon forget that in this world
I exist. Because I do not want you
To call me to your mind when you are dull
And thinking of me, feel anger; I want
To be a dream, be an imagined thing
To be like the dead, ruined flowers we saw
The day before last, one petal—then two—
Trembling and timid in front of the wind
They fell to earth, they were ground into mud.
Yes—passersby trod on them, they are mud . . .
To become mud, though, that is to be clean—
While my existence, half-alive, half-dead
Is really torment. Eyes looking at me
Are full of scorn, saying, "Poor—unwanted—"
Ah, heaven! Why come then? Why come? . . .

I can't forget you. The day that you came—
Like a traveler in darkness, I saw light;
You're my teacher, the one from whom grace comes,
My love, who taught me about love, and life;
From stupor, you shocked me to wakefulness, you
Returned innocence to me and it's because
Of you that I know heaven's high, grass green.
At this moment, you stroke my heart, it leaps
And then you stroke my face—scorching, it burns;
Lucky the night is black, no one can see—
Lover, I'm panting, can't breathe; don't kiss
Me, not now—I'm in flames; can't bear
My life—the fire—the heat—
My soul is on an anvil, blazing hot
Hammered, hammered, with love's hammer, the sparks
Fly, scattering—I'm fainting—hold me! . . .
Oh, love, just let me in this garden's peace
Close my eyes, die in your arms, how lovely.
Above my head, in the white poplar trees
The hoarse voice of the wind will sing my dirge,
Blowing from olive trees, and wafting in
The scent of pomegranate. And that scent
Will waft my soul away, till in the light
Made by the eager, passionate fireflies
I'll halt my steps upon that three-arched bridge
And listen, as you kiss me, call my name,
Shake me, and hold my corpse—still warm.
Smiling, I'll go away then with the wind,
And follow it to heaven or to hell—
Where doesn't matter, so long as I leave
This loathsome life. Truly, to die for love—

To die in the midst of love—that's worth more
Than five hundred rebirths. Selfish, I know
But I don't care. So—won't you die with me?
What?—We must be together or its not
A real love-death. You need two wings to fly.
Just one won't do. It has to have a mate.
And, even if I enter Paradise
I can't be without you. I need your care.
You need me, too. And if I am in Hell
And I'm alone, you will not be at ease.
You say, Hell is not cultured like this world—
That, I do not believe. But still a flower
Like myself, delicate and frail, might meet
With strong winds there; be beaten down by rain.
I'd call for you—What if you could not hear?

That would mean that I had jumped into mud
Trying to free myself. And ghosts would laugh
Ice-eyed, like humans with their icy hearts—
Laugh at my fate; and your weak carelessness.
If this is right, what is there I can do?
It's hard to live, but death won't set me free.
Do not give up your future for my sake—
Ah! I do not want that, and yet it's hard.
You say to wait, wait for another day;
Will that day come? You're here, I feel at peace
But at daylight you go. And are you calm
Deserting me? I could not go from you
So easily. But that is my hard fate.
Yet this flower, with no sun, no sweet dew
Won't die; but it's petals are withering—
How pitiful! You won't forget me, love,
And except in your heart, I have no life.

So yes, I'll listen to your words, I 'll wait—
Yes, till the tree of iron blooms, I'll wait
In patience, love. And forever, you'll be
The fixed star that shines bright above my head.
Should I perish, I will change and become
A firefly, within this garden here,
Close to the grass I'll sink and hide and fly—
Fly from dusk to midnight, midnight to dawn.
I only want the sky quite free of clouds
When I look up, at the lovely large light
Brilliant in heaven. You.
I want you to shine much more brightly, then.
Across the night; across the sky, connect
Us with Love's Inspiration…

—JULY 11, 1925, IN THE MIDST OF THE

HILLS NEAR FLORENCE

This is the title poem of Xu's second published collection and is set, of course, in Florence, Italy, at the time as exotic a place to his Chinese readers as was Cambridge, England. It is a dramatic, psychological monologue heavily influenced by Robert Browning (whose *Dramatic Monologues*, 1842, include *My Last Duchess*, and the *Soliloquy in the Spanish Cloister*). Xu's ability to adapt Browning, and to write a poem completely colloquial and yet so poetic, shows the point to which he mastered his craft. It also shows his ability to create character solely through dialogue, and his skill with the voices of women. Not just the female protagonist but her lover, who does not speak, become real to the reader in these lines. For interesting comparisons see *Late At Night* (p. 103) where the man deliberately does not answer his accusatory companion, and *Coral* (p. 85) where the drowned lover (whose sex is not recorded) cannot speak or respond, but only sigh.

In spite of the alien genre and foreign setting, Xu's work, as usual, is very Chinese, extensively employing Buddhist symbolism and imagery. Note that hell in this poem is not considered permanent; one might escape. There can be five-hundred rebirths; one can hope to be reborn, perhaps as a firefly, an image often employed by Xu. Here it is clear why: She is already figuratively on fire. Other imagery favored by Xu is very developed here—the stars, the moon, the pure flower in the mud, clouds, and wings to fly with, to name just a few. Yet the poem is also very specifically set in Florence, with not just architectural features mentioned, such as the Ponte Vecchio (the "three-arched bridge"), but the scents of olive and pomegranate. The Brownings, of course, had eloped to Italy and it was a place Xu thought and wrote about long before he actually visited it.

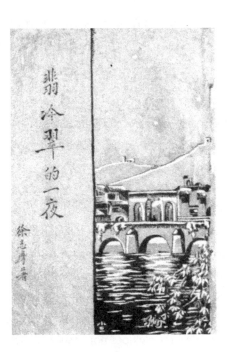

Cover of Xu's 1925 poetry collection, A Night in Florence.

GRIEF

Sadness

悲 思

Sadness is in the front of this courtyard.
　No; for look
　New dreams foolishly dance
　Butterflies love and bees debauch
　The wisteria spits forth beauty
Sadness is not in the front of this courtyard.

Sadness is in the sky.
　No; for look
　Blue and long, white and vast
　Clouds and birds returning, dancing;
　Cosmos of bright air—
Sadness is not in the sky.

Sadness is in my brush.
　No; for look
　Long bristles, white and clean
　Waiting to write and express
　The many thoughts I have inside me—
Sadness is not in my brush.

Sadness is in my paper.
  No; for look
  It's essence pure, though filled with lust—
  Resembling in shame and in anger
  Sentimental longing, sexual desire—
Sadness is not in my paper.

Sadness is surely inside my—
  heart—
  My heart like an ancient mound
  Covered with rootless weeds
  My heart like a frozen spring
  Ice blocking up the living fountain
  My heart like an insect when winter comes
  In hibernation—its mouth stopped—
No! Sadness is not in my heart!

[1923]

Childless

无儿

night

gloom

pigeon

in nest

moans;

feathers

fly

above

pine grove—

This pigeon's trembling

Like a soft child's hand

Trembling when held—

Against breast;

Tickle—loving—

"Pigeon—

Don't move don't move

My heart grieves grieves

My tears flood flood

Pigeon—

Don't move don't move

Childless—I—

Can't bear my mourning."

[1923]

Xu Zhimo's son Peter died in 1925 at age three, so this moving poem about the loss of a child, published in a magazine in 1923, cannot be about his death. The child was living in Germany with his mother at the time.

THE CLOUDS IN YOUR WESTERN SKY

In Front of Exeter Cathedral

在哀克刹脱教堂前

This is my shadow. Reflected, this evening
In the court of this church in a strange land—
A strange and silent shadow, still and lonesome,
A huge and solemn building, cold and grand.

I ask the image in front of the temple,
"Who is in charge of this strange life of man?"
The crumbling old stone statue stares, bewildered—
Even seems angered by my strange demand.

And then I turn to ask the evening star, ascending cold and huge behind the spires of the church. And in mockery it winks—my riddle unanswered in its starlight.

An ancient tree stands near me and he sighs, then.
A mournful sound, as cold as autumn rain
In the empty cold court, while in his shadow
The war dead lie entombed; guiltless, though slain.

For a century now he's seen the changes
That take place in this world. He knows them all.
The tricks life plays on us in the four seasons;
Spring's joys—and the decrepitude of fall.

He knows, this tree, the ancients in this village,
Saw them christened, as children with gold hair;
Saw their weddings at the church door, will see them
When their names are carved onto tombstones here.

> He wearied long ago of this sad farce, this goitered tree. He stands here, unattached.
> And I sigh, in sympathy with him, as the speckled leaves fall on my shadow.

JULY, 1925

133

On the green of Exeter Cathedral stands the Devon County War Memorial designed by Sir Edward Lutyens and put up in 1921 to honor 11,600 young men killed in the carnage of the Great War, still a raw memory in 1925. Although colonized China was a minor participant and so much less affected, the soldiers of World War I were Xu's exact contemporaries (he was born in 1895). The "unattached" tree in the last stanza may be taken in the Buddhist sense of "non-attachment," although Cyril Birch thinks that it represents Thomas Hardy, a poet Xu much admired.

Stanzas three and seven in the original are metered but unrhymed, in contrast with the rest of the poem, which has rhyme and seems more formal. I therefore set them off with italics and and did not put them into quatrain form (though they are quatrains in the original). This poem is also discussed on p. 21 of the Introduction.

*Devon County War Memorial and Exeter Cathedral, photo by Harry Mitchell,
Wikimedia Commons.*

In 2008 a memorial stone inscribed with the first two and last two lines of Xu Zhimo's most well-known poem, *Cambridge, Farewell Again*, was installed at King's College, Cambridge. A browser search of "Xu Zhimo Cambridge memorial" will bring up numerous articles and videos about this popular pilgrimage destination, visited by tens of thousands of Chinese tourists annually. Photo courtesy of Ms. Soo Martin.

Cambridge, Farewell Again
再别康桥

I came to you softly, Cambridge.
And softly I say goodbye.
I wave a hand in a soft farewell
To the clouds in your Western sky;

The gold willows on your river's banks—
Are the twilight sun's new brides,
And their lovely shadows in the lights of the waves
Move in my heart like its tides.

In the soft mire under the water,
Green plants swagger luxuriantly
In the gentle waves of the river Cam
I gladly a plant would be.

That pond in the shadow of the elms
Not a clear spring, but heaven's rainbow—
Colors crumbling in algae white as milk
Drizzling rainbow dreams below;

Looking for dreams?—grasp a punting pole
And through green grass punt upstream,
Stars' radiance will fill your boat
In those stars' refulgence—sing—

But I hear no flutes, no pipes tonight
And I have no voice to sing.
Even the insects seem struck dumb
On this summer's evening—

In silence I came to you, Cambridge,
In silence I say goodbye;
I shake my sleeve as I say farewell,
And I take not one cloud from your sky.

[1928]

If you mention Xu Zhimo's name to a Chinese, this is the work they will begin to recite—or even sing—to you. *Zai Bie Kangqiao* is the poem that they studied in their schooldays, whether in China or Taiwan, and non-Chinese who have heard of Xu will be familiar with some translation of it. The poem's first and last two lines are inscribed on a monument to Xu at King's College, Cambridge University, and it has been translated in many anthologies and scholarly publications, as well as on internet sites. It has been set to music many times now, by both Chinese and Western composers and has been sung as both a classical music selection and as popular songs.

Cambridge, Farewell Again is a beautiful poem in its original language. Xu's great lyric gift is on full display, with its liquid and lovely lines; its haunting, memorable images; and its masterful use of repetition, rhythm, and rhyme. I have translated it in nineteenth-century style verse, as that is the style that Xu actually wrote it in, which would have sounded very exotic to Chinese readers at the time. Most readers (many modern critics excepted) prefer their poetry to be beautiful, and the poem fits well with the widespread image of Xu as "China's Keats," and as an idealist and romantic (discussed in the Introduction, p. 23).

However, *Cambridge, Farewell Again* is more than just a pretty poem, as critical studies show (see Annotated Bibliography). It is both structurally and philosophically complex, simultaneously evoking traditional Chinese poetry and English Romantic poetry, creating a thought-provoking interplay between the two cultures, with many possible meanings and layers. Michelle Yeh (*Modern Chinese Poetry*, p. 100) sums up one possible meaning well, when discussing the poem's "circularity" and how at the end "the dreamer is awakened, the songs are silenced" and how "The poem's return upon itself drives home the underlying tone of disillusionment and despondency." As noted also in the Introduction, however, in Xu's work things are not what they first seem to be, and the poet's words cannot always be taken at face value.

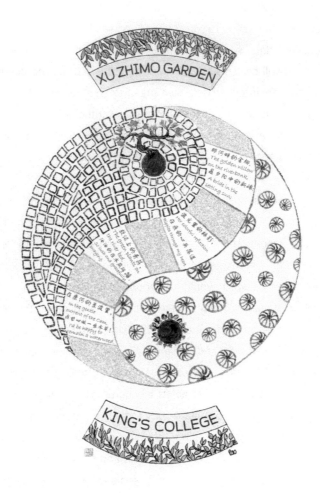

In 2018 the Xu Zhimo Memorial Garden was established adjacent to the memorial stone. Drawing courtesy of Lily Pao Hsu, wife of the poet's grandson, Tony S. Hsu, who dedicated the garden.

To—

给—

I don't remember Vienna;
I remember you, Alice.
Frankfurt, I don't recall,
Except for Dorothee—
Nice; Florence; Paris
All without meaning now,
Only your loveliness remains
Mathilda, Josephine, Renee—
Lithe and light-footed,
Tireless, graceful—
Shining in memory's blackness
Bright stars on a winter's night;
A summer evening's darting fireflies—
How could I not be intrigued and
Intoxicated by my fascination—?

[1931]

In this poem Xu compiles a list of foreign places and women's names that
sound incantory and beautiful in Chinese. As in other poems, the women of
Xu's memory are figuratively transformed into fireflies or bright stars.

BROAD SEA AND EMPTY SKY

I Have One Love

我有一个恋爱

I have one love
I love the bright stars in the sky
I love their crystalline clearness
    Such strange divinity, not of this world.

In the cold of late winter evenings
In the loneliness of grey mornings
On the sea, on mountaintops after storms
    Forever shine one star; myriad stars.

Grass and flowers intimate beside mountain streams
Joyful children, high in towers;
Compasses; lantern lights for travelers—
    Flickering spirits endless miles away; so far.

I have a broken soul
Like broken crystal scattered in heaps on the ground
Among the dead grass in the wilderness,
    Sated with sips of your solicitous flashes.

This world's icy coldness and soft warmth
I tasted formerly and formerly endured.
Sometimes in autumn, crickets' voices under the stairs
    Have wounded my heart, forced my tears to fall.

I have laid forth my honest confession,
Offered love to a whole sky full of brilliant stars.
Whether this life is real or an illusion,
Whether the world continues to exist or is destroyed,
    In the vast universe forever shine unwavering stars.

[1925]

A Faint Spark of Flame

一星弱火

I am alone, and halfway up a mountain.
The peak in front of me, among ascending clouds.
I do not know what kind of bird is near me
Mocking the confusion in my soul.

The white clouds one by one fly upwards,
Transform the distance in its boundlessness,
Inside of my constricted heart, though,
Clouds of worry condense; misery's fog.

The clean, bright morning light comes out, then.
Washes the peak, like a green isle, in front.
And like dull phosphorescence in tomb ruins
Inside my breast there is a small, faint spark.

And this dull and faint spark of a flame
Shining in wreckage and in ash,
Will carry on for a long time more
Though traces of the past still mock.

[BEFORE 1925]

Go Away

去吧

Go away, World, go away!
I stand alone on a mountain summit,
Go away, World, go away!
I face the endless sky.

Go away, Youth, go away!
Be buried with sweet grass growing in a lonely glen,
Go away, Youth, go away!
Mourn with a twilight flock of crows.

Go away, Dreamland, go away!
I drop and I break the jade cup of illusion,
Go away, Dreamland, go away!
I laugh as I receive the respects of the mountain wind and the sea waves.

Go away, all things, go away!
In front of me the high summit pierces the sky
Go away, everything, go away!
In front of me is endless endlessness.

[1924]

Onward, Forward

迎上前去

I won't shun suffering, God, to come to You.
So willingly consign my flesh to flame
Until the last, when I achieve my aim
And can stand, God, on what I know is true—

Penglai is not my goal; nor immortality—
I am content to be a man and earth's enough for me.

[1925]

The meaning of the characters translated "God" in this poem is somewhat ambiguous. *Shangdi*, literally the "Supreme Lord," was an indigenous Chinese deity, but this name was later borrowed and used to signify the Christian God, especially by Chinese Catholics. It does not seem that Xu was a Christian believer, though he was familiar with Christianity and some poems use Christian imagery, such as angels (he uses the English word transliterated for them) or Biblical stories, like a 1923 dialogue he wrote between Adam, Eve, and the snake (not translated here); and *Calvary* (p. 165). In others, like this one, the vocabulary is ambiguous and might be either Christian or refer to Chinese folk or Daoistic beliefs. "Penglai" in the last couplet is a mythical island of the blest, a kind of Daoist heaven.

Of No Importance

卑微

Of no importance
the reed that doesn't resist
the wind that blows.

Withered its semblance,
empty its heart.
How can it make music now?

It prays to the wind:
"I can endure it.
Knock me down."

And then—disintegration
As—uprooted—it drifts
toward the horizon.

[1930]

Unexpected

偶然

I'm a cloud in the sky
Casting a shadow on that pulsing wave, your heart—
No need for surprise
Less need to like
This trace of shadow that shifts and vanishes, quick as an eyeblink.

You—me—meet on the ocean when the night's black
As we travel our different directions—
If you remember, well, great—
But better still if you forget
The light we made together as we met.

[1926]

After *Cambridge, Farewell Again*, this is the poem most loved by English trans-
lators of Xu, and it is very popular in China, too. The title is often translated
Chance or *By Chance*. The latter is not a bad translation but *ouran* has here,
I think, more of a meaning that something happens that you didn't expect,
rather than that it happened accidentally, though probably Xu intended the
ambiguity.

In Search of a Bright, Shining Star
为要寻一个明星

I ride a blind, lame-legged horse
Whipping it towards the black night;
Whipping it towards the black night
I ride a blind, lame-legged horse.

I race into black, unbroken night
In search of a bright, shining star;
In search of a bright shining star
I race into the black, barren void.

I've exhausted, exhausted my mount
And that brilliant star hasn't appeared;
The brilliant star has not appeared
I am so exhausted. Exhausted.

Crystal light pierces the turning sky
Above; my horse falls in the void—
In the black barrenness its corpse lies—
While, crystal, the light pierces the sky.

[1924]

A Little Poem

小诗一首

I admire and envy
The courage he has
That little light
That penetrates the dark.

He only has
A glint of radiance
But does not ask
How deep the universe.

So small and faint
That light of his
So lonely in
The anxiety of black night.

[1931]

You Were In His Eyes
他眼理有你

I climbed up to the highest mountain ridge,
And tore my clothes to tatters on the thorns;
Looked out at the vast realm of windblown cloud
And I did not see you there, O Lord God!

I pierced the thickest part of the earth's crust,
Destroyed the snakes' and dragons' ancient nest,
And in those endless depths, I cried aloud
And did not hear you answer, O Lord God!

I saw a child by the side of the road,
Vivacious; gorgeous in his tattered clothes.
With love in his eyes, he called for his "Ma!"—
And I saw you then in those eyes, Lord God.

NOVEMBER 2, 1928, SINGAPORE

This poem takes up some thoughts expressed in *A Child's Thought of God* by Elizabeth Barrett Browning, a favorite poet of Xu.

Broad Sea and Empty Sky

阔 的 海

Broad sea and empty sky I have no need of.
And I have no wish to release a huge paper hawk
To fly up to heaven and harass the winds in all directions—
      I just want a minute
      I just want a flash of light
      I just want a crevice that's tight;
   Like a child climbing up to a window sill
   In a dark room lying in wait there and
   Gazing up at the sky to the west and the undying cre-
vice, light-
flash, mi-
nute.

[1931]

The "paper hawk" is a kite with a string trailing off at the end, reflected in the shape of this poem (an effect more obvious in the original Chinese characters). See Introduction p. 30 for more comments.

Singers and Heroes

Little Bird

雀儿,雀儿

Little bird, little bird,
You came inside my door
Now you want to go
Bang! You bump your head
On the glass again—
Dim inside this room
In the courtyard, sun
(*And I'm in the room and you don't like that*)
In the courtyard you'd see
Your friends and family.
I open up my hands
And I shout, "Little bird!
I will be your mom
And you my sweet son,
I'll feed you crumbled cake
At teatime every day
And we'll sleep in one bed,
Together dream sweet dreams.
And sing a brand new song."

[1923, EXTRACTED FROM XU'S ESSAY
"A FAIRY TALE," 童话一则]

News from Heaven

天国的消息

Lovely autumn scene! Voiceless, the falling leaves
Fall lightly, lightly on this little road
And from behind the fence comes children's laughter.

Clear sound; embracing the quiet of cottages
Like birds in a dark glen rejoice in morning
Dispersing darkness for limitless light.

And joy emerges, like night-blooming cereus.
My mood becomes carefree; I forget my spring love,
And this life's brevity, regret, worries and sorrows—
Heaven is in the laughter of a child!

Evening clouds flood the golden maple grove.
A chill wind blows at my lone figure, but
In the sea of my soul, great billows surge—
I shout, in answer to that great pulse.

[1925]

On the Train

车上

There are all sorts of people on this train
Soldiers, merchants, youths, infants, bearded men,
Some stand close, some lie down, some close their eyes
Or, eyes open, gaze at the dark outside.

No stars, only train lamps illuminate
The tiredness on each passenger's face
Whether old or young; meanwhile the noise
Of the wheels on the track, an iron voice.

Then, suddenly, a sound issues forth
From one of the corners, deep and dark,
Like a bird greeting dawn, a mountain spring
Or golden rays piercing desert ravines.

She's just a child, delighted with her song
On this blind journey, in this confusion
And like a mountain spring, a bird at dawn
She sings, until the train fills with the sound—

Marvellous music; on each rider's face
Can now be seen joy, and also—surprise—
Soldiers, merchants, men and youths alike
Even the infant opens his eyes wide.

She sings, sings till the road seems filled with light
The moon comes out of clouds, the stars shine bright
Flowers like lanterns on their branches sway;
Swinging on fragile grass stems, glow-worms play.

[1930]

155

On the Trans-Siberian Railway:
Memory of Composing a Song on a Reed Pipe at
Autumn Snow Monastery, West Lake

西伯利亚道中忆西湖秋雪庵庐色作歌

In front of Autumn Snow Temple
In a reed field under the autumn moon,
I picked a round, fat reed up
And tested my flute's new sound.

The moon was a whirling jade fragment,
The field another temple of the gods,
I played a tranquil tune upon the reed pipe
In front of the temple, lost in my thoughts.

I played a tune about the joy in my heart.
Fresh breeze blew snow upon the reed's smooth breast.
Then, as I played about my plans in my joy,
Ten thousand fireflies in the field flashed.

I remembered the sadness of my life, then.
And I was full of misery inside.
I could hear melancholy in the flute tune
In the water, continual frog cries.

Under the bright moon, the snow on the reeds danced
I pondered the mystery of human life.
I was composing a new tune about that,
But my reed (broken) would no longer play.

The moon was a whirling jade fragment,
The field, another temple to house gods,
I played a tranquil tune upon the reed pipe
In front of the temple, lost in my thoughts.

157

In front of Autumn Snow Temple
In a reed field under the autumn moon,
I picked a round, fat reed up
And tested my flute's new sound.

[1925]

Although Xu is not known to have played an instrument, he wrote about
blowing on a reed pipe in several poems. See *Of No Importance* (p. 147), and
Venice (p. 168).

Cloud Voyage

云游

That day you started your cloud voyage,
Carefree, graceful, unwilling to delay
Or stop at any point in earth or heaven,
Your happiness boundless in freedom;
You didn't see beneath, on humble earth,
A flowing stream—and yet your radiance
Startled his soul awake as you passed
Causing him to cling to your shadow.

But what he clutched was sadness without end,
Because Beauty can't be stopped or delayed
In time and space. He longs for you but you've already crossed
The highest mount to cast your shadow now
On the broad sea. And so he wastes away,
That flowing stream, in prayer and in hope
That one day you will fly back again.

[1931]

Cover of Xu's poetry collection Cloud Voyage,
published posthumously, in 1932.

Sea Rhyme

海韵

"Maiden, solitary maiden
Why are you reluctant to leave
The seashore this evening?
Go home, maiden, go home!"
"Ah, no. Go home I cannot.
I love the feeling of the evening breeze."
On the beach, in the evening mist
There's a maiden with the wind in her hair
Lingering; lingering.

"Maiden, maiden with wind-blown hair
Why do you stay here
On the chilly sea-strand?
Go home, maiden! Go home!"
"Ah, no. Hear now my song.
Great sea, I sing and you accompany."
In the starlight, in the cold breeze
A young girl's pure music lightly pours forth,
Rings high and low.

"Maiden, bold maiden
Now the sky pulls up like a black curtain
Now there are frightening winds and waves
Go home, maiden! Go home!"
"Ah, no. Watch me dance here
Like a sea gull diving into the waves."

In the twilight, on the beach
The slender shadow of a maiden
Twists and whirls.

"Listen to the great ocean in its rage.
Go home, maiden! Go home!
Look at the high waves, ravening like beasts.
Go home, maiden, go home!"
"Ah, no. The waves are not coming to swallow me.
I love the motion of the mighty sea."
Into the water, into foaming waves
A panicked little girl stumbles. And—
Falls—

"Maiden, where are you? Maiden?
Where is your song, so loud and clear?
Where is your graceful shadow?
Bold maiden, where?"
Blackness of night swallows the brilliant stars
There is now, on this beach, no radiance
Waves overwhelm the shore, no dancing on the strand—
Gone is the maiden.

[1925]

This poem is now a popular Chinese song, although with the ending much changed. Xu's original has the maiden disappear (probably die) in the ocean, the creative spirit overwhelmed by the powerful forces that It chooses to play with. In the popular song, the theme is changed to romantic love; the maiden is singing and dancing to attract the questioner, and she doesn't die, rather they go off in a happy, sentimentalized ending. Note Xu's use of the English (or Scottish) ballad form, suited to the fated tragedy.

The Yellow Oriole

黄鹂

A flash of color flies into a tree,
"A yellow oriole! Look!" someone says.
Lifting long tail upward, it makes no sound—
Color illuminates dark foliage—
Like spring's brilliance; like passion; like a flame.

Waiting for song, we passionately hope—
Afraid to startle it. It lifts a wing, breaches
Dark foliage, and transformed to bright cloud
Flies off. It's gone. We don't see it again—
Like spring's brilliance; like passion; like a flame.

[1930]

Elegy for Mansfield
哀曼殊斐儿

I entered a dark valley in my dreams last night
Heard cuckoos, among lilies, weeping blood.
I climbed a mountain in my dreams last night
Saw the sky weep, a brilliant tear; just one.

There is a graveyard outside of old Rome
One hundred years, it's kept a poet's bones.
And then the black wheels of Death's car of state
Came shrieking to a halt near Fontainebleau.

The universe—a passionless machine?
If so, why do our ideals light our way?
But if virtue and truth and beauty reign
Why does the rainbow have so brief a stay?

Mansfield, it was just one time that we met
For twenty minutes that will never die.
Who would believe that your goddess-spirit
Has vanished from the world, like dew that dries.

No! Life's not real, it's *Maya*—illusion—
The Power Above keeps you now, lovely soul.
Your thirty years' sojourn, a flower's brief bloom;
Through tears I see you, smiling, return home.

Mansfield, do you recall our London vow
To meet again, by Lake Geneva's shore?
I see Mont Blanc's white reflection in the waves
And look up at the clouds; and my tears fall.

That year, I first knew what Life's message was.
In dream, I woke to knowledge that love's harsh
Awakening to life makes love mature, and
Death shows the boundary of life and love!

Compassion is a crystal that can't break.
Love is the only path to what is real.
Death is a furnace that in mystery,
Smelts into one the spirits of all.

My grief now flies like an electric spark
To touch your spirit in the sky, so far.
I cast my tears, a message, to the wind
When will I break down that dividing door?

[1923]

The "poet's bones" of the second stanza are those of Percy Shelley, who died
in 1822. See Introduction p. 7 for comments on this poem.

Calvary

卡爾佛裡

Hey, guys, look at that fuss! Where? Over there
At Calvary. They're killing men today;
Two thieves. And there's another—do you know
Who he is? He's a devil, people say,
Others say he's Messiah, God's own son.
Oh look, it's him. There he is, coming now
Ah. Why is there someone who's helping him
Carry his cross? You see—those other thieves
Have their own crosses strapped to their shoulders!
They're following Jesus. Oh. Yeah. Jesus.
Who is he really? People say he has
Authority. You can see that he's kind,
Gentle—Shh! Listen up! He's talking!
He says, "Father, forgive them, they don't know
The sin they are committing here today."
Don't you feel though, it's strange, what he says,
Strange when you hear it? Makes your blood run cold—
That tow-headed thief, look at him, he seems
Like someone waking from a dream, he's pale
And he's crying, look at those great big tears.
He's repented! If he can be forgiven
He's every bit as good as any priest.
Hey, look at those women! Like little lambs
They follow Jesus, too, heads bare, hair loose,
Can't stop bawling, crying out loud as if
Their own dear sons were going to be nailed
Up on a cross. It seems as if they think
The sun will not rise tomorrow morning.

Look, in that crowd down there, the Pharisees,
Pharisees in their long robes and tall hats
Following behind. Such sneaky faces!
So smug! Look how they smile. I can't stand them
Listen to how they yell. "Faster! Climb up
To the Place of the Skull! Quick! Nail him up!"
But who's that there slinking along the wall?
Him? Dark-skinned? Ugly mug? It's that Judas,
His disciple. What kind of disciple?
You know, the one Jesus made treasurer.
They were very good friends a real long time,
Together for years during thick and thin.
Who knew he'd change like this; greedy bastard!
The day before yesterday evening
I heard that Jesus ate with his twelve friends.

Judas was there, still one of them; Jesus
Knew he was going to sell his blood, his life.
While they all ate together, Jesus said
He would give his flesh to feed their hunger
And also give his blood to slake their thirst.
His meaning was that, in adversity,
He wished them to give help. Then, with his hands
He washed their feet. He washed Judas' too.
And used his own waist-cloth to wipe them dry.
Who knew that that dark-faced one wouldn't wait;
Eager to sell his own master for gain!
I heard, that evening Jesus and the twelve
Went to the Mount of Olives for a rest.

And Judas showed the way. The sky was dark
It had just gotten cold. And like when you
Light a fire in the woods, the snakes appear
Judas, more poisonous than any snake
Kissed Jesus on his mouth. That was his sign.
It was Jesus' bad luck. Hurry up. Look
He's bleeding now, his blood is on the cross.
I think you're good, and he's certainly bad
Judas should not be allowed to sell Jesus
Sell him in this dirty way; sell Jesus!
It's horrible, watching how he lets them
Nail him alive to a cross, like a thief,
I can't stand to look! Haven't you heard
The dreadful prophecy? Because I've heard
Once this is done, sky and earth will turn black,
I believe it; sky and earth will turn black—
Let's go home!

[1924]

Venice

威尼市

Standing on bridge
Sweet, hot dusk
Distant flute and lyre—dot, line
Circle, rectangle, square
All brilliant gold
Oblique in waves
Cyrstal blue condensing
Sound of song, gondola
Candlelight gem luster
Dream? like life . . .
　　　—mist, confusion—
Mirage vanishes
Before flowing water's breast—
Lovely colors entangle my mind
Flow flow
Flow entering deep dusk,
My soul, a lyre string
Feels unseen thrusts
Throbs, wavers
Softly moans.
New tune from the gondolier
Comes forth like concentrated
Fragrant smoke
But—
This subtle heart lyre—
Who is there to enjoy it?
Who listens . . . ?

[1923]

In this poem Xu incorporates his Chinese translation of a poem by Friedrich Nietzsche, but there are so many changes and additions that it has truly become an original poem, one with Xu's preoccupations more evident than Nietzsche's. The changes start in the second line with the evening becoming "sweet and hot" rather than the "brown" of the original and continue with the addition of the geometrical shapes "brilliant gold / oblique in waves," rather than just golden drops. Nietzsche speaks of drunkenness while Xu simply of "mist, confusion." But then Xu launches into an extended metaphor based on Nietzsche's simile of the poet's soul as a lyre; Xu feels his "strings" being played by an unseen entity in a much more concrete way than the German, who just speaks of being "invisibly touched."

In his article "Xu Zhimo Dreaming in Sawston (England)—On the sources of a Venice Poem," Raoul David Findeisen asserts that Xu definitely did not use the original poem by Nietzsche but an English translation, which he presents along with his translation of Xu's expanded poem. The article demonstrates that Xu's knowledge of Nietzsche was extensive, and that Xu had not visited Venice when this was written.

Cover of Xu's 1925 essay collection, Self-Analysis.

PROSE
AND TALKS

About Xu as a Prose Writer

Although the focus of this book is Xu Zhimo's poetry, it would not be com-
plete without some mention of his prose. He is as renowned for his diaries, his
letters, and especially his essays, as he is for his poems. "No one in China has
ever achieved the magnificence that Xu Zhimo's essays . . . have," the great
Chinese writer Shen Congwen once said,[1] and while this is high praise indeed
in a nation whose essay writers from centuries past continue to be held in high
esteem, it is now recognized that Xu is definitely one of the twentieth-century
masters, who can be placed alongside Hu Shi, Lu Xun, and Zhou Zuoren. And
he is the only one of these three who is also a great poet.

Twentieth-century prose is revolutionary in the history of Chinese writ-
ing, like twentieth-century poetry, because it is in *baihua*, or vernacular, rather
than in *wenyenwen*, but its evolution was different,[2] and Xu Zhimo was not one
of its pioneers. His prose works are well regarded for other reasons. Fu Guang-
ming, research fellow at the National Museum of Modern Chinese Literature,
expresses what many Chinese feel about them, when he says that they are
"rich in expressing emotions"; "full of poetic rhythm"; "brilliant and complex
. . . with the colorful attractiveness of a painting."[3] His essays, always written

in the first person, range widely in topic as he describes places seen in his travels; reminisces about his childhood; introduces the great European classics (and explains why they are great); talks about people he has met (including many of the key figures of the day); discusses social issues or memorializes his dead friends (as a vast number of others would later memorialize him). He suits his style to his subject but always makes his readers feel that they are sitting conversing with someone who is an extraordinarily keen observer, brilliant at analyzing what he sees but unwilling to force his opinions on others and certainly never polemical, with the rare ability to describe his own emotions and foibles honestly—and laugh at himself in a gentle way, as he laughs gently at others. It is unfortunate indeed that very little of this has been translated into English (even less than his poetry) especially since Xu Zhimo was a true citizen of the world, travelling to places as varied as Japan, India, and newly communist Russia as well as all over Europe during the key interwar period, and writing about these places, not only about China.

These few translations and excerpts will not do much to remedy that situation but may, I hope, give readers a small taste of what his achievements were in this area.

1 Fo Guangming, trans. by Taiping Chang, "The Splendid Chinese Culture: Xu Zhimo," Academy of Chinese Studies, c. 2015. https://en.chiculture.net/?-file=topic_details&old_id=0429 Accessed 10 June 2020.

2 The major difference is that something of a *baihua* prose tradition already existed because of the classic novels. Interested readers can refer to C.T. Hsia's *The Classic Chinese Novel* (1968) for this history.

3 Fo Guangming op. cit.

Autumn Thoughts on the Indian Ocean
印度洋上的秋思

Mid-Autumn Moon Festival last night. A curtain like a screen of mica hung in the Western sky last night at dusk, concealing the brilliance of the setting sun; and the sea and sky became dark blue and tranquil as a black-robed nun at the Vatican saying her prayers. After a while, the wind in the ship's sails and the cables holding them could be heard, making a sound like weeping. The evening clouds, in the misty rain, pressed on the horizon, making the end of the ocean look as narrow as if it were a lake. You could not tell if the black shadow on the side was a cloud or mountain. Traces of tears filled the air over the water.

Another autumn mood! In the sound of the rain as it swiftly galloped in was the feeling of hearing the desolate voice of a reed flute, and in addition a somberness that whispered the word "Autumn!" in the ear of my soul. This gentle infiltration, adding autumn thoughts to the sadness that I had felt in the spring and summer, united with my frustration and gave birth to a sickly child— Sorrow.

Earlier, the sky had turned a deep black, and the rain had ceased. But weeping clouds still loosely curtained the sky, only allowing a little pallid light to appear. Informed in advance, the moon was dressed and waiting for those curtains to be drawn, and the ship spat out abundant smoke in the meantime, creating a long bridge as ornate as an official's robes, which connected the froth on the green waves emitted by the ship with the edge of the western sky. This was illumined from both above and below and seemed as if it was reluctant to be separated from the traces of tears in the west.

Then a bright new star issued forth from a gap in the clouds in the north sky, beautifully dressed, like a bridesmaid, gaily asking the news. The bride herself, though, had not yet come out.

When I was a child, each time the Mid-Autumn Moon Festival arrived, I would stupidly sit at the window upstairs, looking out, waiting to see the "bright halo around the moon." If the sky happened to be misty and cloudy, I would worry that there would not be "crystal clear moonlight." But if it happened that I could see luminescent twilight clouds, like fish scales, there would be joy in my childish heart. I would send up a silent prayer that the halo around the moon would blossom soon rather than late—I had heard that cirrus clouds mean a moon halo. Invariably, however, before the moon began to shine, my mother would send me up to bed. Therefore, the halo has remained something that I have imagined, but not actually seen, until this time.

The sky is full of layers of cirrus clouds, now. And in an instant, memories of my early years come back, but my pure childhood innocence—where has that gone?

Moonlight has a mysterious gravitational pull. She can make sea waves roar and she can make sadness come in, like the tide. Under the moon sighs can coalesce into mountains; under the moon pure tears can cultivate acres of orchids, thousand of blossoms, like bright purple jade. I suspect that sorrow is a congenital part of human heredity. If it is not, why is it that years can pass without a reason to grieve and still sometimes, in a rush of shining glory, our tears fall?

But I cannot weep tonight. It's not that I have no tears nor is it because the fact that I'm civilized and educated has eliminated my natural instincts. Rather, it is because when I feel psychological sorrow it arouses inquisitiveness and rationalism in me and I want to study Chateaubriand's dissection of this "melancholy."

On such a romantic moonlit night, though, it would be inhumanly unfeeling to enter into cold analysis . . .

I didn't go looking for the moon in order to search for the sensations of autumn, and I was definitely not seeking new sorrows. To deliberately immerse oneself in sadness is something that Dante says is a sin. It's that I sense the mood of autumn when I look at the moon and when I look out of an autumn window, I feel sad. Humans are such fragile bundles of nerves!

To return to the scenery, though: The autumn moon was lightly wrapped in cloud brocade, like a maiden covered with a veil, luminous in beauty and bright in appearance like a bride. The threads of her veil were violet grey, the color of a lotus root. She hesitated as she entered, through the traces of tears. The hesitation of a lovely girl. Hence, I say:

> *Autumn moon—*
> *I do not hope for your loveliness.*
>
> *...*
>
> *Autumn Moon—*
> *Who can afford*
> *The romantic strokes of your silver fingertips—*
>
> *...*
>
> *Meandering black smoke—*
> *Felicitous autumn moon—*
> *Blackness warming chilly eyes and cold heart.*
> *Coldly puts on festival garb,*
> *Comes to attend—*
> *These joyous nuptials; this funeral.*

[1922]

Here I have translated the beginning of Xu's essay and then skipped to excerpts from the end, for the sake of including the lovely fragments of a poem embedded in it. The essay was written on Xu's return journey to China by steamship after four years abroad, first in the U.S. and then in England. Mid-Autumn Moon Festival is one of the important Chinese holidays, associated with the moon goddess Chang O (see my book *Repairing the Sky*). But even more than this, autumn is the proper season to reflect on the transience of life, and autumn melancholy is a widespread literary trope. "Melancholy" however, was not, in Xu's time, a Chinese word; he transliterated it from English after his reference to Chateaubriand. The phrase he used for the sounds of the word, 眸冷 骨累 (*Mou leng gu lei*) literally means "cold eyes and weary bones," hence his reference in the poetry at the end to "chilly eyes" being warmed.

Sunrise on Mount Tai

泰山日出

We were on the summit of Mount Tai, having just completed an ocean cross-ing, looking at the sun coming up from beneath the Pacific horizon. This is not an unusual occurrence and I have seen incomparable sunrises over rivers, seas and the Indian Ocean. On mountain summits, though, and especially on the heights of Mount Tai, we naturally expected that sunrise would be different from usual. With innocent curiosity, we hoped for something special, and indeed, when we first began to look at the still dark sky, the west was iron-green, while the east was tinged with white. It seemed formless and empty, a vast void. But this was probably because my sleep-filled eyes were not yet com-pletely open, and I felt the fierce dawn chill. When my spirit returned to my body from wandering in sleep, I could not help crying out. In front of my eyes was something I'd never seen. There had been a storm, all the previous night.

And the storm had created an ocean of cloud. Except for Sun View Peak, and the spot where we stood on Jade Emperor Peak, there was diffuse cloud essence everywhere. The rising sun had yet to appear, and the clouds were like an infinite amount of sheep with curled horns, sleeping on top of each other, with their backs together. I stood alone in the midst of that endless cloud sea, as if on an island, and began to imagine strange things—

My body began to grow to a limitless size; the mountains underneath my feet gave shape to my torso, which was a stone fist. A giant with disheveled hair stood upright on the mountain peak and faced the east, stretching out his long arm in the hope of uniting, in exhortation, and in tears which had been hidden up until now, and in the age-old longing of those tears was mingled joy and sadness—

These tears aren't shed in vain; this silent prayer is not without an answer.

The giant stretches forth his hand, Eastward—

What is that unfolding in the East?

In the East, there are fabulously beautiful, glorious colors. From the East comes a huge universal brilliance, to bless everyone—it's appearing—it's arrived—it is here—

Rosewater, the pulp of grapes, redwood sap, agate essence, frost covered maple leaves—myriad dye workers working in layers on the clouds, countless creeping ichthyosaurs crawling into the pale heap of the white clouds—

A place of varied color, uncovering the drowsy sky, calls forth the bright clouds in all directions and the bright steed of the sun enthusiastically gallops forth—

And the ocean of cloud also awakens so that a wave of clouds, shaped like a sleeping beast, is now brought back to life with a great cry. Rearing its head, waving its tail, this wave heads towards our ephemeral, dumpling shaped island (dyed a green color), and rinses over it, stirring up sprays of water on all four shores, shaking the floating reef of this life as if to tell of the coming of life and joy.

Look again to the East, at the muscular sea which has already washed all hindrances away, and at the golden clouds like a barrier of birds, which come forth on its limitless shoulders, expanding now to the earth's edge!

Rise up! Rise up! Exert your strength! Exert your strength! A circle of pure flame leaps out from the horizon, pushing away the clouds so that the blue sky shines forth—

Sing!

Praise!

This is the resurrection of the East!

This is the victory of light!

The giant scattering forth prayers, his body of myriad colors stretched out on the limitless sea of clouds has now begun to vanish in the universal rejoicing.

Now his magnificent ode is also becoming again imagination, in the bright clouds, though it penetrates everywhere.

Listen—to this joyful voice penetrating everywhere.

Look—at this universal shining light!

This is my imagination right at this moment of sunrise on Mount Tai, and also my song of praise looking forward to Tagore, coming to China!

[1923]

From *Xu's Preface to Tyger*

猛虎集序文

. . . There was a time when my poetic feelings were truly similar to torrents of water pouring from a mountain, gushing wildly in every direction. That was during the first half year that I wrote poems. My life had received a great and heavy shock and there was regret, so the half-ripe and unripe ideas that I grasped and considered all dispersed themselves in profusion like a rain of flowers. At that time, I had absolutely no model to pattern myself on, and I did not worry about this. In my heart and mind there was an accumulation of ornate things which I got rid of by allowing my wrist to randomly put them in order. It was as if I had a need to do this, in order to save my life. So how could I consider what was beautiful and what was ugly? In a short time, I wrote a great deal, but practically none of it was ever seen by anyone else. It was an apprenticeship.

The poems in my first book, *Zhimo's Poems*, were all written in the two years after my return home in 1922. In that volume, my feelings no longer, like water, came frothing out the way that they had done at first but there was still no poetic artistry or technique to speak of. This problem continued until 1926 when Yiduo and I and a group of friends had just started a poetry supplement in the *Chenbao Fujuan*. Yiduo is not only a poet—he is a person who enjoys talking on a deep level about the theory and art of poetry. I think that in the past five or six years all of our group of poet friends have been deeply influenced by the author of *Dead Water*. Originally my brush was the wildest stallion and wouldn't accept bridle or rein; only after I saw Yiduo's carefully done, strict work did I awake to the truth about my own wild spirit, but my unconventional temperament would not allow me to follow the detailed rules that Yiduo and others proposed for poetry...

[1931]

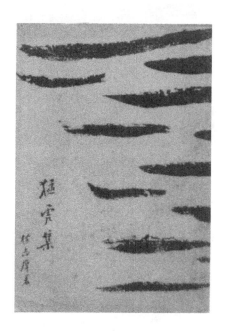

Cover of Xu's 1931 poetry collection, Tyger.

In this preface to his third published collection, Xu mused upon his earlier work, looking back on everything that he had published up until this point. Here are excerpted his thoughts on what he called his "apprenticeship," well as his thoughts on his first volume, *Zhimo's Poems*. *Tyger* was titled after the poem by William Blake, which Xu translated as part of this collection. The Chinese use the "wrist" as a synecdoche to mean the act of writing in the same way that we use "hand," as it is believed that the strength of a calligrapher is contained in the wrist. Wen Yiduo, a friend of Xu Zhimo and another member of the Crescent Group (the "poet friends"), was another important May Fourth poet, famous for his collection *Dead Water*. (The stagnant water symbolized China at that time.) As mentioned in the preface, Xu Zhimo was the editor of the *Chenbao* (*Morning Post*) literary supplement, which published many works in the new vernacular writing style, and his comparison of himself (here, his pen) to an unbroken horse was one he made often.

A Conversation One Night: A Real Old-Style "German"
一宿有话剧: 真正老牌 "迦门"

In the evening, when I get on the train, my baggage is made up of cigarettes, candy and honeyed tangerine wine.

In the pullman car, there are two beds; mine on top, his on bottom.

"You're Japanese?"

"No."

"Chinese?"

"Yes."

"Do you drink whiskey? Huh?" (He means soda, not really whiskey.)

"Thanks very much, no. I'll smoke."

"Are you going to stay in Paris long?"

"No."

"I was an officer in the army—the German Imperial army."

"Really? So, then, you saw combat?"

"From the beginning to the end. I was in a total of 72 battles."

"A hero! Who did you fight? The British?"

"I fought on all fronts."

"How many men did you kill?"

"Three thousand French, one thousand British."

"Who were better fighters?"

"The British. The French aren't too good."

"Why?"

"Drink too much. Too much womanizing."

"So you killed them. And you don't respect them. But what about the French women? You must have had a lot of opportunities."

"Ugh—how many would you want? They aren't too clean, you know. You know, they don't bathe enough."

"Smutch! Ha, ha! But some of them are pretty, hey? Although they don't match the women of your great nation—do they."

"Uh, there are pretty ones. But that doesn't make any difference. They won't do. They aren't healthy. They are diseased—you know? It won't do."

"You fought in so many battles; weren't you wounded?"

"Yes, look." (He takes off his nightshirt, opens his undergarments and reveals his deformed shoulder. The arm seems to have been broken, it has had a hole scooped out of it, the skin is twisted and wrinkled; it's ugly and peculiar-looking.)

"You're all right now, though?"

"Ah—see for yourself—" (He stretches out his arm, makes me feel an iron-hard bicep.) "I'm a boxer."

"How were you wounded?"

"A shell exploded. I was standing and the shell burst right in front of my face, I quickly spun my body around this way."

"Did you fall?"

"I didn't even totter."

"But—you went to the hospital?"

"Yes, I was in the hospital five weeks. Then I convalesced at home another five weeks. This was at the end of 1917. In January the next year, I went back to the front again. And I killed a lot more French."

"You were in the infantry?"

"Yes. Infantry. I used a tank."

"How'd you fight the French? Wasn't it frightful on the field?"

"Fought them face to face, then side by side, then exploded in the middle of them. I captured thirteen big ones."

"Did you fight the American soldiers?"

"No. We fought the French blacks. They couldn't fight—were easier to trap than crows."

"Have another smoke, please. What's your job, nowadays?"

"I'm in business. The clothes business. What you see me wearing, it's from my own shop."

"Would you fight again?"

"Of course. Watch, within ten years, Germany will defeat England and France."

"How will you fight France?"

"The Russians might help us. They could fight Poland first, then the French right flank would be undefended."

"Then you're bound to need help from the Chinese."

"Not bad. Not bad. Germany, Russia and China will unite, turn the world upside-down, France will be *kaput*, Japan *kaput*, America *kaput*, and as for England, you won't need to bring them up again."

"You don't like the Japanese, either?"

"No, the Japanese won't do. They themselves have no culture—culture belongs to China and Deutschland. The Japanese are monkeys."

"Have some honey wine, please. Drink to our future victory, as allies."

"Pour another glass for me."

"Do you have a family?"

"Are you asking if I have an old lady? No, no—if you have a family, you have no freedom. I'm a businessman. I'm here today, gone tomorrow; if you have a family, you are—" (He can't think of a word.)

"Handicapped."

"Ah, not bad—handicapped! Want to see how good my health is? You have a knife?"

(He lowers his head to unfasten the little knife hanging from my watch-chain; I can see the top of his bald head. There are three big scars on it. It looks like the head of a venerable old man. I can't help laughing.)

"What's funny?"

"I'm laughing about the French." (By this time, he has already opened the little knife. He asks me to feel the blade to see if it's sharp. I'm baffled.)

"Is the knife sharp?"

"It's sharp."

"Now look." (He stretches out his right leg, expels a breath, and takes the knife in his hand. He holds it up high, the sharp edge down and slashes the blade against his thigh. There is a bizarre sound, and the knife flips onto the floor, as if it had struck metal. He repeats this.)

"Amazing! You're a real man. But you don't like women?"

"Ah—sometimes. When there are a lot of women, one spends money. Their love—ha! ha! But fighting is much more fun. Much more interesting than women."

"I believe it. So you just want to fight again? Your political party must be the Deutschland Nationalist Party."

"Of course. You see the three-colored party badge that I wear."

"Who do you think has a chance of winning this next election?"

"Victory will be ours. General Hindenburg is really great."

"You admire him?"

"One hundred percent."

"Great! Let's toast again—your party's victory!"

———

"Yesterday evening there was a good play in Berlin—did you see it?" (he asks).

"*Oscar Wide?* That was the opening night; I'm upset that I didn't go. Did you go?"

"I went."

"Was it good?"

"Not bad. That business about Wilde—do you believe that?"

"Maybe. He could have been curious."

"Curious? I think it's a way that people are born. Does it exist in China?"

"Naturally there are exceptions like that in every country. What about Germany?"

"It's very stylish. There's nothing strange about it. It's in the schools, in the army, in Berlin there are clubs—you know?"

"I didn't know that. So you all really don't think it's strange."

"Not at all. Come to München for a while. You'll know."

186

"Ah. You Germans really are a great race! But now it's late. Time to rest. Goodnight."

—Zhimo, Written in the hills near Florence
on June 7th, 1925

This is an example of the prose that Xu Zhimo published frequently in order to allow Chinese readers to experience the West along with him. It is also interesting as an early description of a member of the National Socialist German Worker's Party, long before the "Nazis" appeared to be a serious threat. (There were many nationalist parties in post World War I Germany, but the "three-colored" badge describes the NDSAP's distinctive red, white, and black.)

Xu presents the ex-soldier entirely through dialogue, using words sometimes written in the Roman alphabet for color: "Oscar Wide" [sic], "handicapped," "tank" "München." There is no commentary—readers are allowed to reach their own conclusions about this man, but in an explanatory note attached to this piece, Xu explains that he doesn't believe that this particular German is typical. He has a German friend, he tells the reader, who is much more representative, adding: "He also fought in the war for four years, but he really hates war. He's a deep thinker, who studies hard and loves peace—a farsighted, honest, likeable young man. It's a shame that what one learns early enters into one's bone marrow, though, and that it's hard then to deviate from it by even an inch. If you wanted to write a description of my friend, it wouldn't be easy—not simple like describing this man, who exposed himself as soon as he opened his mouth . . . Do you think that the art of slashing at one's thigh with a knife will catch on in polite society?"

From Leisurely Talk While Staying in the Hills Near Florence
翡冷翠山居閒話

Here, in the warm April evenings, when you go out for stroll, whether you climb uphill or go down, it seems as if you are going to a feast, or entering an orchard where every tree has the most luscious fruit hanging from it. When you cease to be satisfied with standing still and looking, you have only to stretch out a hand and pluck—to taste the fresh flavor, to satisfy the drunken confusion of your soul. The sun is warm, but not too warm; the breath of the wind wafting in from the flowery mountain groves, often brings a scent of the woods. This exquisite scenery makes it seem as if a painting on canvas had come to life in front of your eyes . . .

[1925]

188

From *My Grandmother's Death*

我的祖母之死

> *— A simple child,*
> *That lightly draws its breath,*
> *And feels its life in every limb,*
> *What does it know of death?*

This quatrain is the beginning of the famous poem by William Wordsworth called *We Are Seven*. It expresses the meaning of the entire poem. The poet, who loved children and nature, once met an adorable eight-year old girl with curly hair and asked her how many siblings she had. She replied: "We are seven." She told him that two were away in the city, two in a foreign country, and that one sister and one elder brother were buried in the cemetery near her home. However, in her child's heart, she didn't recognize that there is a difference between the living and dead, and thus every evening she carried her supper to a grassy place in the graveyard and ate and sang there alone. She sang for her brother and sister resting in the grave beside her. Although they were quiet and made no reply, in her innocent childish heart, she did not realize that there is an insurmountable barrier between life and death. And therefore, despite old Wordsworth's repeated explanation, she simply opened her eyes wide and kept replying: "But sir, we are still seven people."

Wordsworth himself could not escape the same conclusion as this little girl. He had formerly admitted, "During my childhood I could not believe that one day I myself would also quietly lie in the grave, and that my bones would become dust." On another occasion, he told someone, "When I was a child, I couldn't understand that such a thing as death would one day come to me, also."

Children are curious by nature: they want to know why the cat eats mice; where little brother comes from; or which comes first, the chicken or the egg.

However, the greatest change in life, the phenomenon and reality of death, they comprehend only vaguely. We can't expect children to be like Hamlet, with his speculations. When they attend a funeral, children will often weep along with the adults, but once their tears dry, they run to the garden to play at shuttlecock or chase butterflies and continue to do this even when the beloved one who is sleeping in the house won't wake up, whether it is father or mother, older brother or sister. We cannot assume that their mourning will eclipse their childlike joy. When you say to a child, "Your mother is dead," most of the time he will simply stare at you in confusion; but when he calls and she does not reply—there will be tears on his cheeks, then. But the way that children naturally express themselves is often what's most moving. One of the most memorable things I ever saw was a scene from a movie depicting a child's love for her dead mother. She saw flowers being planted in a garden, and the gardener told her that that if they were watered, the flowers would come up out of the ground. It rained heavily that night. She was awakened from sleep by the sound of the rain. Suddenly, she remembered what the gardener had said, and an idea came into her mind. She crawled out of bed in secret, went downstairs and into the study, where she took the photograph of her dead mother which was on a table. Holding it in her arms, she walked out into the garden in spite of the falling rain. She dug the soil up with the gardener's little spade, and then carefully took her beloved mother in her arms, planted her in the mud and covered her. After she finished, she knelt there, waiting—a three- or four-year old in white pajamas, kneeling on the ground in the pouring rain in the middle of the night, waiting for her dead mother to grow, like flowers and grass, out of the soil!

My first encounter with the great misfortune of a close relation's death was more than twenty years ago, when I was not yet six years old and my grandfather died. This was my first dreadful experience, but when I recall how I thought about it at the time, I was not much different from Wordsworth's little girl, so far as how I regarded death. I remember that night the family informed us that Grandfather was severely ill, and that they were not going to sleep that night but that my sisters and I should go upstairs to bed and that

A teenaged Xu Zhimo at home in Xiashi, Zhejiang Province.

if things changed, they would come and call us. We went upstairs and my grandfather's bedroom was right underneath. I didn't quite understand what was going on but I knew that something frightful was happening that night: a fire, a burglary, some fearful nightmare. I couldn't sleep soundly because of the noise of hurrying footsteps below us; the dishes banging; maids calling out; weeping—constant sounds. After midnight they came, while I was still dreaming, carried me downstairs in their arms. I woke up and heard the weeping. They had begun to burn the incense and the whole room was full of smoke, full of people pressing around the bed, sobbing and crying aloud. It was soon my turn, too, to look at my good grandfather lying on the big bed, in all that crowd. Suddenly, I heard him sit up. There was a pause in the weeping, and I saw my father climb onto the bed, take my grandfather in his arms and hold him against his breast. Grandfather leaned on him. His eyes were closed. There was a piece of black medicine in his mouth. He spoke very softly and I couldn't hear him; later I was told that he was unconscious for a few seconds but then awoke and said to his family, "You're frightened; it was only a faint." He went on to say a few more words in a low voice before he left us and did not revive again, but I didn't see the end with my own eyes. Or maybe I just don't remember. I just remember kneeling on the floor for a long time, holding an incense stick in my hand, and following the others, bawling loudly.

NOVEMBER 24

Xu goes on to speculate on the meaning of life and death, then describes his grandmother's passing. He concludes with a translated quotation from William Cullen Bryant's *Thanatopsis*, contrasting with the opening Wordsworth quote. Although no year is given, Xu's grandmother died sometime in the early 1920s.

From *Fallen Leaves*

落葉

The day before yesterday, your Mr. Cha telephoned me and asked me to come and give a speech. I said that I had nothing to say and that, furthermore, I don't have the patience to give speeches. His reply was, "Come; you have total freedom to say what you like. Our students' lives are full of melancholy; listless; dry. We want you to come and give us a little living water." What he said moved me. Listlessness, melancholy: these are things that I know about. I don't know you gentlemen well but the fact that there is sadness in your emotional lives connects me with you, gives me a deep feeling of fellowship. I know what kind of a strange thing depression is: shifting, shapeless—something that you cannot clearly describe. When it comes to a person, their whole body feels trapped, as if caught in a spider's web. If you struggle, you can move; say, stretch an arm out, but you cannot become unstuck. It is a very frightening web. I also know what listlessness is like. Its eyes and its disgusting countenance. I think you all also know it. There is nowhere that it is not. It attaches itself to a person's body, sits on their face—Look at your friends as they pass, their faces all show its presence. Look in the mirror. I think you will each see it there. Horrifying languor: it's like a poison; once it gets inside of our veins all of our sensations change and even our flesh changes in color. And we fear that the new color is that of leaving life—of approaching the grave.

I am a person who believes in feelings. Perhaps I was created to be emotional, from my birth. To give an example of how I am affected by things, the west wind blew in during these past few days. The morning that it blew in, I awoke feeling frozen, and saw that the color of the paper in the windows was more than usually pale. My limbs, in their nest of blankets, felt as if they had been doused with cold water. I heard the sound of the wind outside the windows blowing in the jujube trees among the dry leaves; I heard it blow those leaves down one by one. They blew around in the courtyard, and they made a hoarse kind of sound; some flew outside, but some stayed circling in a corner of the wall and the noise that they made really seemed like sighs. The western wind, then, waking me cold out of my dreams and stripping, scattering, the leaves off the trees seemed terrible to me. His success in a hungry, poor and miserable society seemed tragic. When I went outside later that day, nothing on the street was the same. The old men laboring so hard, the children huddled on street corners shivering—early or late, I realized, they would all meet the fate of the dry leaves. That day I felt extremely anxious, extremely depressed.

For this reason, when I heard Mr. Cha say that your lives were so sad and so dry, I understood and I wanted to come and speak with you a bit. My way of thinking—if it can be called a way of thinking—has never been systematic. I don't have the ability to be like that. My intelligence is of the impetuous kind—you might even say that I arrive at my ideas in a painful and convulsive fashion. When thoughts do not come to me, I can't make them come. When they do come, it's as if I'm wearing soaking-wet, uncomfortable clothes and *must* think of a way to take them off. An example—what I just told you about the dry leaves in the autumn wind. My thoughts can be compared to the leaves on the trees; when the time hasn't arrived, they won't fall. When the time comes though, they just need the strength of the wind and they fall downwards, one by one. Perhaps most of them already have no life: are dry, are burnt. However, among these will be some few, perhaps, who still have traces left in them of autumn's colors. The maple leaves, for example, may still be red. The leaves of the cherry-apple trees may still be multi-colored. These leaves are absolutely of no use, but some people, like myself, have a fondness for them. When they first fall, the color is fresh, but as time passes, that color will change, unless you preserve the leaf well. And my words, that is to say my thoughts, are useless also most of the time, but sometimes they, too, retain some of the colors of life. If you don't love them greatly, you can trample them at your will as you pass; you don't have to pay attention to them. But perhaps there are a small number of people whose fate this is. Do not call them useless—perhaps, unexpectedly they may take what they've collected and have embraced in their arms, putting some inside of a book, with the hope of prolonging and saving the hidden, tranquil colors.

Feelings, genuine feelings, are rare and valuable. They are what everyone should have. We mustn't cut off feelings or suppress feelings, that action is a crime; suppressing the source will not stop the flow and perhaps it is a crime like strangling children, cutting off their breath. People in society are not, naturally, mutually connected. Feelings, both innate and acquired, are a kind of thread which make a warp and woof and take separate individuals and weave them into a whole that has hidden meaning. But there are occasionally times when the threads rot, or become lax, and therefore a society must continually produce new threads, remove and repair the rotted places and tighten the places that are slack in order to mostly preserve the integrity of the fabric. Occasionally, the ability to produce increases a great deal and we then have the opportunity either to extend or increase the surface we already have (or make it more dense, like double-stringing a tennis racket).

Since we know the force necessary to create or destroy this self-made fabric, our society, the force necessary to make more of it or to burst it—God's force and Satan's—actually already exist in it at the same time. It is not often that these two different kinds of force balance equally, as on a scale. Usually, if one side doesn't drop, then the other does. And truly, if humanity's destiny is being weighed on one side of a balance scale, you can see that a giant black shadow counterbalances us on the other side. This shadow is the embodiment of our ability to unite together. His hands are heavy with the weight of the standards that he clutches and distributes, now here, now there. And the terrestrial globe, revolving to its greatest extent, and the sun, the moon and the stars all shine in their turn, while our fate is being weighed in this way, on this scale.

Just now, I spoke of tennis rackets. This is a good analogy in another way— those of you who play tennis know that there are a few strings on a racket that are most important and play an essential role. Sometimes, if these few strings are very sturdy, not only can you seize the ball, whip the ball, bounce the ball against your opponent with remarkable force—but your racket can stand up to further hard use. A minority of exceptional elements preserve the integrity of the whole entity.

And this is why I say that feelings are so valuable . . .

[1924]

Wordsworth
"Lucy Gray, or Solitude"

"葛露水" Jan 31 1922

我常聞名葛露水：
我嘗路經曠野
天　時偶　遇見
這孤獨的小孩。

無伴，露水絕少相識．
她家在一荒涼的倨厓
—— 一顆最希有的珍珠
偶尔 掉落人間呀！

Partial manuscript dated January 31, 1922, of Xu's translation of
Lucy Grey, *by William Wordsworth.*

Xu as Translator

Translation, in general, is not so difficult as the translation of poems.
The difficulty in translating a poem lies not just in its form and also
not just in its spirit and its rhyme, but in the fact that you must take
the spirit and rhyme and change them to fit a new form in the way that
the colors in paint change when they touch water. You must also let the
form manifest the spirit and the rhyme in the same way that a delicate,
exquisitely made bottle complements the perfume inside.

Some translations of poems adhere especially rigidly to form,
using the original number of words, rhyme, etc., that were used in the
model. More often than not though, the poem's spirit and flavor then
become superficial. Others especially emphasize the spirit and senti-
ment. The result then is most often the writing of a completely different
poem, one that has, unexpectedly, strayed too far from the original. In
this case, it can't be called a translation at all . . .

[FROM *A Question of Translation*, AUGUST 23, 1925]

In a book of translations of Xu's poems, it seems fitting to present Xu him-
self as a translator.[1] In my opinion, he was extraordinarily adept, at his best,
and he was at his best most of the time. I have seen his version of Christina
Rossetti's *Song*,[2] to give one example, anthologized in Chinese as an original
poem—it reads so smoothly that I suppose the Chinese editors assumed that it
was originally Chinese.[3] Yet the poem so accurately renders Rossetti's English
that I was stunned. I recognized it for what it was immediately. Not only is the
meaning the same as Rossetti's meaning, but the translation is in her style—
rhyme, rhythm, stanza divisions, and everything else were the same— and Xu
managed to retain her lyricism.

But Xu seems to have tried to do this in most of his translations. He tried to reproduce the style of the poem— what he called its "spirit"—he did not just translate the bald meaning of the words, as is so often done nowadays (in what are called "scholarly translations"). He also did not invent his own entirely new poems, using the original poet's idea as a starting point, as all too often happens in the translations that we say are poetry in their own right.[4] Thus, when Xu translated Walt Whitman (a section of *Song of Myself*), he not only reproduced Whitman's meaning— he wrote in a virile and rugged style. When he translated Tagore, he wrote discursively, like that poet. He managed to do this even with Shakespeare. Xu's miraculous rendition of the balcony scene from *Romeo and Juliet* is so Shakespearean that it even gives the impression of being in blank verse. It is not, of course, as that would be impossible in Chinese; what Xu uses is the flexible 11, 13 syllable line that he had perfected and used for his poems *Cricket* and *A Night in Florence*. The dialogue between the two lovers in the translation is poetry in Chinese, very beautiful poetry. Yet, once again, accuracy was not sacrificed. It could be translated back into English, almost word for word, and the meaning would be the same as Shakespeare's.

At times, Xu did choose to change the form of a poem. An example is his version of Keats' *To a Nightingale*, which he translated as a prose poem, incorporating it into one of his most famous essays. My literal translation of Xu's Chinese would be: "This singer, the one singing this marvelous song, absolutely isn't an ordinary bird; she's definitely a beautiful forest goddess that has wings and can fly." This would strike any reader familiar with the original English as not very much like

> . . . thou, light-winged Dryad of the trees.
> In some melodious plot
> Of beechen green, and shadows numberless,
> Singest of summer with full-throated ease.

Xu encountered difficulty here, though, expressing what a "dryad" is in a language disconnected from Greco-Roman traditions. It was easier for him to present William Blake, as he did with his rendition of *The Tyger*. This retains the original meaning and is definitely a Chinese poem, though it lacks, I think, Blake's brilliant, disjointed expressiveness. Xu used it as the title piece of his collection *Tyger*, though, and it is very effective.

It is interesting to look at the poems Xu selected for translation. His choices are further proof of what is discussed in the introduction—that he was not primarily a "Romantic" poet. Keats, Wordsworth, Blake are all represented, but twenty-two of the sixty-seven translations that Liang Ren presents—about one-third of the total—are from Thomas Hardy, confirming Cyril Birch's opinion about the influence of this poet on Xu. There are four translations from Katharine Mansfield.[5] Then there are translations of Victorian poets still popular in Xu's lifetime but now obscure—men such as Edward Carpenter, Arthur Symons, and James Elroy Flecker. I have not been able to locate the originals of several of his translations at all. Who is the "Rosemary" who wrote something called *The Bright Moon and the Nocturnal Moth?*[6] Xu also sometimes took poems that he liked out of novels and translated them. He did five poems by Friedrich de la Motte Fouqué, for instance, taken from the novel *Undine*, using the English translation by Edmund Gosse.

De la Motte Fouqué originally wrote in German.[7] Xu's primary foreign language was English, and he seems to have translated almost entirely from English—on the occasions when he did translate from other Western languages, he seems to have used English translations. Thus, he translated Sappho and John of Tours by way of Dante Gabriel Rossetti, and Omar Khayyam by means of Edward Fitzgerald. He did Schiller and Goethe—I don't know whose translations he used. It seems, though, that he did read French.[8] Possibly his translation of Baudelaire's *Une Charogne* was a direct translation. He also wrote an essay on this poem, which he called *Sishi* (死屍), meaning "corpse." Xu's translation of Baudelaire is interesting because the French poet was a symbolist. So Xu had an interest in this style.[9] He translated Walt Whitman, also, but the poet who wrote such works as *Broad Sea and Empty Sky* and *Don't Pinch, It Hurts* does not seem to have had any familiarity with the work of such contemporaries as Pound, Yeats, Eliot, or Amy Lowell. Of course, the fact that Xu did not translate them does not mean, definitively, that he had not read them, but it does not seem that he had. In his essays and critical writings, when he speaks about European poetry, it is with reference to the Romantics, Swinburne and Matthew Arnold, Tagore, or his favorites, Hardy and Mansfield.[10] According to Michelle Yeh, later Chinese poets in the 1930s and 40s, such as "Bian Zhilin, Shi Zhecun, Yuan Kejia, Mu Dan, Zheng Min and Du Yunxie introduced Chinese students to Anglo-American poets and critics including T.S. Eliot, W.H. Auden, I.A. Richards, and William Empson, and ushered in the Modernist canon."[11] Xu, of course, died before this happened, in 1931, but his *baihua* poetry had laid the foundations.

One final fact is that Xu did some translations from classical Chinese into the vernacular, including a selection from the *Classic of Poetry* (*Shijing*, 11th–7th century BC). He also translated twelve works by the poet Li Qingzhao (c. 1084–1155), who was one of the great Chinese poets—and a woman—again showing his interest in women and poetry.

NOTES

1 The texts I used for this essay were from the sixty-seven translations by Xu included in *The Complete Edition of the Poems of Xu Zhimo* (*Xu Zhimo Shi Quan Bian*), Liang Ren, ed. Zhejiang Artistic Press, 1990, pp. 395–542.

2 "When I am dead, my dearest, / Sing no sad songs for me . . ."

3 The error appears on p. 195 of *Selected Works of Xu Zhimo* (*Xu Zhimo quan ji*), published by Jiangmen Cultural Publishing House, Taiwan, 1988, 12th reprint 1997.

4 The exception to this is the poem *Venice* (p. 168) discussed in the endnote following it. Liang Ren did not realize it was based on a translation and included it with Xu's original poetry.

5 Mansfield wrote little poetry, however. Xu translated a great deal of her prose.

6 Xu's translation (明月與夜蛾) is quite lovely.

7 De la Motte Fouqué was prolific but known today mostly for the novel *Undine*.

8 See Chang, Pang-mei Natasha, *Bound Feet and Western Dress*, Doubleday, 1996, p. 103.

9 At least one critic, Victor Vuilleumier, believes that Xu was "a Chinese symbolist." See "Xu Zhimo's Encounter with 'A Jewish Nightmare': How a Chinese Symbolist Viewed an Expressionist Yiddish Play," in *Studia Orientalia Slovaca*, June 26, 2020, pp. 145–55.

10 Xu translated poems of both Swinburne and Arnold as well.

11 Yeh, Michelle, *Modern Chinese Poetry: Theory and Practice Since 1917* (Yale University Press, 1991), p. 18.

Xu Zhimo's signature and seal.

Index to Poems and Chinese Titles

A Night in Florence

204

Painting by Lily Pao Hsu illustrating the world travels of Xu Zhimo.

Annotated Bibliography

Birch, Cyril, "English and Chinese Metres in Hsu Chih-mo." Institute of History and Philology of the Academia Sinica, vol. 8, 1960, pp. 258–293.
An invaluable technical analysis, although Birch's metrical understanding of Xu is controversial.

Birch, Cyril, "Hsu Chih-mo's Debt to Thomas Hardy," *Tamkang Review*, vol. 8, issue 1, 1977, pp. 1–24.
Enlightening and convincing.

Birch, Cyril, ed. *Anthology of Chinese Literature, Volume 2: From the 14ᵗʰ Century to the Present Day.* Grove Press, 1972, pp. 341–355.
Harold Acton and Ch'en Shih-Hsiang first translated and published poems of Xu Zhimo in English in 1936, but Cyril Birch was the first to translate Xu based on an in-depth study of his work (see his "English and Chinese Metres" above). His literary criticism of Xu, and his translations of a few of the poems and of the essay "The Cambridge I Knew" are important.

Bonett, Dorothy Trench, *Repairing the Sky: Tales of Myth and Magic from Old China.* Create Space, 2017.
Retells Chinese myths and legends key to understanding many Xu poems, both thematically and in their use of imagery.

Cao Xueqin (1715–63), *The Story of the Stone*, David Hawkes and later John Minford, trans., Penguin Books, 5 vols., 1974–86.
For his excellent English-language translation, David Hawkes used the alternate early title of the great Chinese novel more widely known as *Hong Lou Meng* (紅樓夢, *The Dream of the Red Chamber*). See commentary on *Listening to the Piano Late at Night* (p. 107) for the relevance of this book in understanding Xu Zhimo.

Chang, Pang-Mei Natasha, *Bound Feet and Western Dress.* Bantam Books, 1996.

Chang is the great-niece of Zhang Youyi, Xu's first wife. Youyi's reminiscences are included here, creating a dual biography spanning generations.

Collins, Martha, and Kevin Prufer, eds., *Into English: Poems, Translations, and Commentaries*. Graywolf Press, 2017, pp. 113–120.
    In seven brief pages, Bonnie S. McDougall compares the Kai-yu Hsu, Michelle Yeh, and Hugh Grigg translations of *Cambridge, Farewell Again* with the original Chinese and analyzes what each conveyed and what each left out in order to render the poem into English. It gives those who do not read Chinese an excellent idea of what Xu's poetry is like.

Fairbank, Wilma, *Liang and Lin: Partners in Exploring China's Architectural Past*. University of Pennsylvania Press, 2008.
    Chronicles the marriage and achievements of Lin Huiyin and Liang Sicheng as the first Western-trained architects in China, and also discusses Lin's relationship with Xu and his influence on her (as confided by Lin).

Findeisen, Raoul David, "Xu Zhimo Dreaming in Sawston (England)—On the sources of a Venice Poem" *Asiatica Venetiana: Revista del Dipartimento di studi indologici ed estremo-orientali dell' Universita Ca' Foscari di Venezia*, vol 1 (1996) pp. 27–41.

Fo Guangming, trans. by Taiping Chang, "The Splendid Chinese Culture: Xu Zhimo," Academy of Chinese Studies, c. 2015. Retrieved 6/10/2020 from https://en.chiculture.net/?file=topic_details&old_id=0429

Fung, Mary M.Y. and David Lunde, trans. *Selected Poems by Xu Zhimo*, Mary M. Y. Fung, ed. The Chinese University of Hong Kong, 2017.
    Accurate translations of a large number of poems and of his three prefaces.

Hsia, C.T., *The Classic Chinese Novel: A Critical Introduction*. Columbia University Press, 1968.
    The best basic introduction to the six classical novels, including *Dream of the Red Chamber*, revered by Chinese readers.

Hsu, Changhsu Hamilton, see Xu Zhimo.

Hsu, Kai-yu, "Hsu Chih-mo," in *Twentieth Century Chinese Poetry: An Anthology*, pp. 69–96. Anchor Books, 1964.

> Author Hsu (no relation to the poet) has translated sixteen poems by Xu Zhimo for this anthology, adding a partial translation of another, and reprinting five by Cyril Birch. It includes a lyrical essay on the poet's life and influence.

Hsu, Tony S., *Chasing the Modern: The Twentieth Century Life of Poet Xu Zhimo*. Cam Rivers Publishing, 2017.

> This well-researched biography by the poet's grandson includes family photographs and information available nowhere else, and is important reading for anyone with an interest in Xu Zhimo. It is fascinating to read in tandem with Gaylord Leung's *Literary Biography* (see below).

Lee, Leo Ou-fan, *The Romantic Generation of Modern Chinese Writers*. Harvard University Press, 1973.

> Lee, who has been influential in understanding Xu Zhimo, believes him to be the great romantic of modern Chinese literature, part of a "romantic generation" that lost out to Communism.

Leung, Gaylord Kai-Loh, *Hsu Chih-mo, a Literary Biography*. PhD diss., SOAS University of London, 1972.

> The pioneering biographical work on Xu in English. It complements the work of Tony S. Hsu.

Leung, Gaylord Kai-Loh, *The Poetry of Hsu Chih-mo*. MA thesis, University of British Columbia, 1969.

> Incisive literary criticism and excellent analysis.

Liang Ren (梁仁), ed., *Ai Mei Qiao Yu, Xu Zhimo Qing Shu* (爱眉悄语,徐志摩请书, *Whispers of Loving Mei: Xu Zhimo's Love Letters*). Zhejiang Artistic Press, 2000.

> Xu Zhimo's love letters to Lu Xiao Man, and their diaries, from 1925 to 1931, edited by Lu Xiaoman and published after Xu's death.

Lin Hui Yin, *Lin Hui Yin Wen Ji* (林徽音文集, *Collected Works of Lin Hui Yin*), Liang Cong Cheng (梁從誡), ed. Taiwan: National Library, 1990.
> Xu Zhimo wrote some of his greatest poems for Lin Huiyin and influenced her to write poetry. (She is also considered a member of the Crescent School.) This collection contains two of her essays memorializing him, as well as poetry, some written in response to his. I have translated one of these pairs (pp 107–11).

Lin, Julia C., *Modern Chinese Poetry, An Introduction*. University of Washington Press, 1973.
> This book is like a course on modern Chinese poetry from 1917 to 1972. Lin translated nineteen of Xu's poems completely and partially translated five. Her literary criticism is enlightening (though I do not agree with all of it) and her analysis sensitive, presenting important material about his stylistic development and the influence of classical Chinese poems on his work.

Liu Fu You (刘福友), ed., *Xu Zhimo Daibiao Zuo* (徐志摩代表作, *Representative Works of Xu Zhimo*). Hunan People's Publishing Co., 1994.

Liu Yan Sheng (刘炎生), *Xu Zhimo Ping Zhuan* (徐志摩评传, *Criticism of Xu Zhimo*). Jinan University Press, 1996.
> In addition to important biographical information, this book gives a good idea of what criticism of Xu Zhimo was like in mainland China twenty-five years ago, when his reputation began to be rehabilitated there.

Liu, James J.Y., *The Art of Chinese Poetry*. University of Chicago Press, 1962.
> Appreciation of Xu's contribution to modern Chinese poetry is enhanced with some knowledge of traditional Chinese poetics, and Liu's slim guide is the best available in English.

Lösel, F.A.G. "Friedrich Nietzsche's *Venice*: An Interpretation, in *Hermathena* No. 105, Autumn 1967, pp. 60–73.
> This essay includes the Nietzsche poem on Venice that Xu incorporates in his poem of that title.

Ma Xuecong, *Crescent Moon School: The Poets, Poetry and Poetics of a Modern Conservative Intellectual Group in Republican China*. PhD diss., University of Edinburgh, 2017.

> Although this is a doctoral thesis and reads like one, Ma has a unique and convincing view of the Crescent movement (that they were conservatives) and she highlights the importance of Xu in this key literary movement.

Pan, Lin, *When True Love Came to China*, Hong Kong University Press, 2016.

> Chapter 14, "Exalting Love" has some interesting insights on Xu Zhimo.

Spence, Jonathan, *The Gate of Heavenly Peace: The Chinese and Their Revolution, 1895–1980*. Penguin Books, 1982.

> Spence uses Leo Lee and Gaylord Leung as sources, so does not present information on Xu that those do not contain. It is still highly recommended as it presents in a marvelously lucid and readable style a history of Xu's turbulent times and the personalities who influenced it.

Wang, Zilan, *Xu Zhimo, Cambridge and China*. Exhibition catalogue, 2014.

> This bilingual (English and Chinese) catalogue was created for the 2014 exhibition of the same name held in the King's College Antechamber, Cambridge.

Wen Mu (文木) and Yu Hua (郁華), *Xu Zhimo Xin Chuan* (徐志摩新傳, *A New Biography of Hsu Chih-mo*). National Library, Taiwan, 1996.

> This popular biography of Xu Zhimo and the women in his life does not add much to the understanding of his poems, but does offer insights into how some readers understand them.

Wu, John Jr., "Bosom Friends: Hsu Tse-mo and My Father," *A Collection of Articles Presented in the Seminar for the 2000 Academic Year*, pp.129–42. Department of English Language and Literature, Chinese Culture University, Hwa Kang, Yangmingshan, Taipei, July 2001.

> John C. H. Wu was Xu Zhimo's closest friend. John Wu, Jr.'s recollections of Xu as seen through his father's eyes are historically important, as well as enlightening.

Xu Zhimo, *Feilengcui shan ju xianhua* (非冷翠山居閒話, *Idle Talk While Staying in the Hills Near Florence*). Storm and Stress Publishing, Taiwan, 2018 reprint of the 1927 edition.

> One of Xu's collections of essays, some excerpted in Yang Mu (below).

Xu Zhimo (Changhsu Hamilton Hsu), "The Status of Women in China," MA thesis, Columbia University, 1921.

Xu Zhimo, *Xu Zhimo quan ji* (徐志摩全集, *The Complete Works of Xu Zhimo*), Jiang Fu Cong (將復璁) and Liang Shiqiu (梁實秋), eds. Taipei: Biography Publishing House, 1969.

> Liang Shiqiu was a founding member of the Crescent Group and very close to Xu Zhimo. Zhang Youyi was consulted for this early edition.

Xu Zhimo, *Xu Zhimo shi quan bian* (徐志摩诗全编, *The Complete Poems of Xu Zhimo*), Liang Ren (梁仁), ed. Zhejiang Artistic Press, 1990.

> This is the edition I used for most of the translations, although I also looked at editions from Taiwan.

Xu Zhimo, *Xu Zhimo quan ji* (徐志摩全集, *Complete Works of Xu Zhimo*), Han Shisan (韓石山), ed. Beijing, Commercial Press, 2019.

> This recent edition in ten volumes, which I did not have access to, is at present the most complete edition of Xu's work in Chinese.

Xu Zhimo, *Xu Zhimo quan ji* (徐志摩全集, *Complete Works of Xu Zhimo*). Taipei, 2000.

> This Taiwan edition of Xu's complete works adds writing discovered after the 1969 *Complete Works* edited by Jiang Fu Cong and Liang Shiqiu (above). It has some works not included in the *Complete Poems* edited by Liang Ren that I used as my main source.

Xu Zhimo, *Xu Zhimo sanwen xuan* (徐志摩散文選, *Selected Essays of Xu Zhimo*), Yang Mu (楊牧), ed. Taipei, 1997.

> Includes many of Xu's essays from various sources, some from *Idle Talk* (above).

Yeh, Michelle, ed., *Anthology of Modern Chinese Poetry*. Yale University Press, 1992, pp. 5–12.

Translations of nine poems, and a partial translation of another, very accurately rendered.

Yeh, Michelle, *Modern Chinese Poetry: Theory and Practice Since 1917*. Yale University Press, 1991.

Yeh is the greatest living expert on modern Chinese poetry. This book is organized by theme; Xu Zhimo is not its primary focus but there is a lot of discussion of his work interspersed with information on other major modern Chinese poets, and Xu's influence on some of them. I recommend especially the analysis of how Xu used "circularity."

Floating World Editions publishes books that contribute to a deeper
understanding of Asian cultures.
Editorial supervision: Ray Furse. Editorial consultant: Tony S. Hsu.
Book and cover design: Liz Trovato. Printing and binding: IngramSpark.
The typefaces used are: Schneidler Initials, Goudy Old Style, and Frutiger.

CPSIA information can be obtained
at www.ICGtesting.com
Printed in the USA
BVHW040450170221
600304BV00004B/9